roads and trails

OF OLYMPIC NATIONAL PARK

By FREDERICK LEISSLER

Published in cooperation with the
Pacific Northwest National Parks Association

SEATTLE   *University of Washington Press*   LONDON

PHOTO CREDITS

National Park Service, by Gunnar Fagerlund: title
page, 1, 4, 5, 6, 7, 8, 9, 13, 14, 15, 19
National Park Service, by Bob Haugen: 2, 16
National Park Service, by Carsten Lien: cover, 3,
12, 17
National Park Service, by Neil Mortiboy: 18
National Park Service, by George Grant: 11

The mountains can be reached in all seasons. They offer a fighting challenge to heart, soul and mind, both in summer and winter. If throughout time the youth of the nation accept the challenge the mountains offer, they will help keep alive in our people the spirit of adventure. That spirit is a measure of the vitality of both nations and men. A people who climb the ridges and sleep under the stars in high mountain meadows, who enter the forest and scale peaks, who explore glaciers and walk ridges buried deep in snow —these people will give their country some of the indomitable spirit of the mountains.

—William O. Douglas
Of Men and Mountains

1. Graywolf Ridge and the Needles

PREFACE

Olympic National Park is a paradise for all who love the outdoors. In deep forests, along rivers and ocean shores, on alpine ridges, and through mountain meadows, its many scenic roads and its more than 600 miles of trails promise physical adventure and spiritual tranquility. There are short trips, long trips, easy ones and difficult, in variety sufficient to suit nearly everyone's time, ability, and inclination. This book will help you select and plan trips and will serve as your guide while you are in the back country.

The park may be divided into three major sections. The first division is the east side of the park. The eastern Olympics are high and rugged and drop abruptly to Hood Canal, which is an arm of Puget Sound. Roads penetrate up the valleys, and where the roads end trails begin, running through virgin forests and along stream banks in narrow valleys to ridgetops and mountain passes.

The second major division is the north side, the most accessible part of the park. Park Headquarters are located at Port Angeles, and the Port Angeles Visitor Center is nearby. This center of information for park visitors was opened to the public in 1957.

Only from the north side can the Olympic high country be reached by car. Here roads lead to the ridgetops at tree line at Deer Park and Hurricane Ridge. Roads run several miles up the Elwha and Soleduck rivers, connecting with trails that lead into the heart of the Olympics.

The third division is the west side of the park and includes the Pacific Coast Area. Several rivers drain this wettest side of the Olympic Mountains and empty directly into the ocean. Spur roads from U.S. 101 push up the valleys and lead to trails that continue through fairyland forests. These are the rain forests that grow in Olympic's broad-floored and gently sloping western valleys, where the annual precipitation is 12 feet. Although the rain forests are exceptional enough in their own beauty, nature has for good measure set them apart as the home of the Roosevelt, or Olympic, elk.

The Pacific Coast Area, a wild, untamed coast, extends for 50 miles along the Pacific shore. U.S. 101 borders the ocean for about 10 miles at the southern end of the strip, and branch roads run to the Indian village of La Push and to Mora and Rialto Beach.

This guide to the park includes a map for each major watershed and Pacific Coast Area. The maps show automobile roads, campgrounds, ranger stations, and trails, as well as mountains, ridges, streams, and lakes. Numbers following place names—as, for example, "Mt. Olympus 7965"—indicate elevation. Trail distances are given in miles and tenths of miles between points on the trails. Most trails have been measured by using a cyclometer attached to a bicycle wheel pushed along the trail, the most accurate procedure. Some trails, especially the way trails, have been measured by pacing.

Distinction is made between way trails and other trails, because the former are rough, or are not maintained. Some park trails are also noted as unsuitable for stock use.

The back country is beautiful and friendly. The wild animals are not dangerous unless molested. It is wise to put your food out of reach of animals, especially bears, at night or when you are away from camp. Hanging your food at least 10 feet above the ground might save you from hunger and harassment. There are no poisonous snakes, and poisonous plants are very rare. Mosquitoes can be troublesome in some places, so it is a good plan to carry an effective repellent. Mountain water is safe to drink—help keep it that way. Some streams along the coast may be contaminated. If you have any reason for doubting the purity of the water, boil it or purify it chemically.

On the trail be comfortable, rest well, and eat well. Do not allow yourself or members of your party to become exhausted by traveling too fast or too far. An average of 2 miles per hour is good hiking time on the average mountain trail. Never try a long hike unless you are in good physical condition. Do not leave the trail unless you are an experienced woodsman and are familiar with the terrain. Plan your trip before you start. You should include a proposed route and alternatives to follow in the event of unforeseen circumstances. Be sure to register at a ranger station and outline your proposed trip to the ranger, giving your estimated time of return and indicating the probability of a change in plans. You will be issued a backcountry use permit. All this is for your protection, and it may be the means of saving your life.

The Olympic Mountains are subject to heavy winter snowfall with attendant heavy runoff in the spring and early summer. Because of variations in snow pack and rate of melting, the trails, especially the higher ones, cannot be opened at the same time each year. Before starting a trip into the back country it is advisable, especially in the early part of the season, to inquire about trail conditions at Park Headquarters or at a ranger station. Write to Superintendent, Olympic National Park, 600 Park Avenue, Port Angeles, Washington 98362.

The numerous peaks in the park offer high adventure to the skilled mountain climber. Inexperienced climbers are advised to stay on the trails rather than to attempt to follow the unmarked routes to the summits. Detailed climbing information for peaks in the Olympics are included in *Climber's Guide to the Olympic Mountains*, by Olympic Mountain Rescue and published by The Mountaineers, Seattle, in 1972.

I am indebted to Justice William O. Douglas for permission to quote from *Of Men and Mountains* (New York: Harper & Brothers, 1950) and to the following individuals at Olympic National Park Headquarters, who made it possible for me to complete this guide: Fred J. Overly, former Superintendent; John F. Aiton, former Chief Ranger; John A. Nattinger, Supervisory Forester; Floyd L. Dickinson, former Park Forester; and Gunnar O. Fagerlund, former Park Naturalist. Thanks are also due to members of the field ranger force who gave valuable aid.

FREDERICK LEISSLER

2. Sunset at Ruby Beach

CONTENTS

ILLUSTRATIONS

Map 1

North Fork Skokomish River

Lake Cushman-North Fork Skokomish River Road

0.0 mi. U.S. 101 at Hoodsport, Washington, on Hood Canal.

4.0 Lake Cushman Resort.

10.0 Junction with state forestry road to Hamma Hamma River Road.

15.0 National Park boundary.

16.0 Staircase automobile campground. In forest setting near river's edge. Stoves, tables, and sanitary facilities.

16.0 Staircase Ranger Station. Information and backcountry use permits. Approach to Wagonwheel Lake Way Trail. End of road.

This area is easily accessible from the towns of Olympia, Shelton, and Bremerton. From Hoodsport the road climbs through cutover forest lands to Lake Cushman Reservoir, which extends to the boundary of the park. The road follows the east shore of Lake Cushman to the park boundary and continues a short distance through the forest to the Staircase campground and ranger station near the beautiful Staircase Rapids. The road ends here and trails begin, leading to the high country and excellent mountain climbing.

Hamma Hamma River Road

This road leaves U.S. 101 15 miles north of Hoodsport and is maintained as far as the Lena Lakes Trail, 8.5 miles up the

Hamma Hamma River. The road actually extends another 7 miles up the river.

Six miles from U.S. 101 is a U.S. Forest Service guard station where backcountry use permits and information may be obtained. There is a U.S. Forest Service camp near the start of the Lena Lakes Trail, with tables, stoves, and sanitary facilities.

Staircase Rapids Trail

0.0 mi. Staircase Area.
3.2   End of trail on Four Stream.
         Approximate hiking time: 2 hours to end of trail.

This trail is through heavy virgin forest along the south bank of the Skokomish River. It passes Staircase Rapids 0.5 mile from the ranger station. About 2 miles further up the river the trail turns west and follows along Four Stream to its end in the timber.

Staircase-Lake Cushman Trail

0.0 mi. Staircase Area.
0.75   Park boundary.
         Approximate hiking time: 15 to 20 minutes one way.

This trail follows the south side of the river to the park boundary and the north end of Lake Cushman. A U.S. Forest Service road crosses through the park on part of this trail.

Wagonwheel Lake Way Trail

0.0 mi. North Fork Skokomish River Road, across the road from
         Staircase Ranger Station.
2.9   Wagonwheel Lake.
         Approximate hiking time: 1.5 to 2 hours.

This is a very steep trail through fairly dense forest.

Mt. Lincoln Way Trail *(not suitable for stock)*

0.0 mi. North Fork Skokomish River Trail, 2.4 mi. above Stair-
         case Ranger Station.

MAP 1   **3**

2.5   End of trail in an old burn.
5.1   Summit of Mt. Lincoln (5868).
        Approximate hiking time: 1.5 to 2 hours to end of trail.
        To the summit a good 5.0 to 5.5 hours.

Mt. Lincoln, located at the south end of the short Sawtooth Range, gives a commanding view of the interior ranges of the park to the west and north. The upper 2.5 miles are covered with brush and fallen logs and should be attempted only by experienced woodsmen.

Flapjack Lakes-Gladys Divide Trail

0.0 mi. North Fork Skokomish River Trail, 3.7 mi. above Staircase Ranger Station.
3.6   Junction with trail to Smith Lake (2.1 mi.).
4.1   Flapjack Lakes.
5.6   Gladys Divide. Start for climbs of Mt. Gladys, Mt. Cruiser, and others in the Sawtooth Range.

This trail climbs through the forest to the 2 lakes which lie near timber line. These lakes contain eastern brook and rainbow trout; there are 2 shelters here. From the lakes it is 1.5 miles to Gladys Divide between the North Fork of the Skokomish and the Hamma Hamma watersheds. On the divide a splendid view may be had of the short Sawtooth Range to the south and of Mt. Henderson to the north. From the divide short climbs can be made to Mt. Gladys and the towerlike summit of Mt. Cruiser (6104).

Smith Lake Trail

0.0 mi. Flapjack Lakes-Gladys Divide Trail, 7.4 mi. from Staircase Ranger Station.
2.1   Smith Lake.
        Approximate hiking time: 3.0 to 3.5 hours.

This trail breaks out into open country soon after leaving the Flapjack Lakes-Gladys Divide Trail. Bears can be seen, especially in the fall when the huckleberries ripen. Mt. Henderson can be

3. Mt. Olympus, Blue Glacier at left

MAP 1   **5**

reached by a miner's trail from Smith Lake and a climb to the northeast.

North Fork Skokomish River Trail

3.8 mi.   North Fork Skokomish River Trail.

5.9   Junction with Six Ridge Trail. This trail leads up the ridge to Six Ridge Pass (9.6 mi.) and then down Graves Creek to the Quinault River Road, 9.0 mi. beyond the pass (Map 16).

6.7   Camp Pleasant.

9.6   Nine Stream.

12.7   Junction with Mt. Hopper Trail to Hagen Lakes (5.0 mi.) and Mt. Stone (5.0 mi.). Mt. Hopper Trail becomes a way trail after 2 mi.

12.9   First Divide (4688). Divide between Skokomish and Duckabush watersheds.

13.2   Home Sweet Home.

15.6   Junction with Upper Duckabush River Trail to Marmot Lake (3.4 mi.), Hart Lake (4.4 mi.), and Lake La Crosse (4.7 mi.). From the junction it is 16.4 mi. to Duckabush River Road (Map 2), 4.6 mi. to O'Neil Pass, 15.2 mi. to Enchanted Valley (Map 16), and 26.0 mi. to Quinault River Road (Map 16).

This trail follows the west side of the river through beautiful stands of Douglas-fir and western redcedar to a short distance below the First Divide. From here to the divide and part way down to the Duckabush River the trail passes through beautiful high-country forest, then through open meadows, and again into the forest.

Six Ridge Trail *(not suitable for stock)*

0.0 mi.   North Fork Skokomish River Trail, 5.9 mi. from Staircase Ranger Station.

5.4   Junction with Lake Success Way Trail to Lake Success (4 mi.).

6.4   Belview camp.

8.5   McGravey Lakes.

9.6   Six Ridge Pass (4600). From the pass it is 9.0 mi. to Quinault River Road (Map 16).

This trail climbs steadily up the south end of Six Ridge through Douglas-fir forest to Belview camp, which is located in an old burn. At approximately the 5-mile marker, a 4-mile way trail leads through meadow and subalpine fir country to Lake Success. From Belview camp to Six Ridge Pass the trail passes through open high country of rough terrain.

Mt. Hopper Trail and Hagen Lakes Way

0.0 mi.   North Fork Skokomish River Trail, 12.7 mi. from Staircase Ranger Station.
2.0   South side of Mt. Hopper and end of maintained trail.
5.0   Hagen Lakes.

This trail contours around the south side of Mt. Hopper through forest and meadow areas to the ridge at the head of Crazy Creek. From this point it more or less follows an elk trail on the south side of the ridge leading east toward Mt. Stone and Hagen Lakes. The view across the upper Skokomish Valley to Mt. Skokomish and Mt. Henderson is breath-taking. This way trail can easily be lost; stay on an even contour to find it again, and follow it around to the west side of Mt. Stone. Turn north over the ridge and follow a valley down to the largest of the Hagen Lakes. The more experienced hiker can make his way cross-country from this lake up over Mt. Stone and pick up the Scout Lake Way Trail leading to upper Lena Lake (about 4 mi. beyond Hagen Lakes) and the trail to the Hamma Hamma River Forest Service Road.

Lena Lakes Trail

0.0 mi.   Hamma Hamma River Road, 8.5 mi. from U.S. 101.
2.0   Lower Lena Lake.
6.0   Upper Lena Lake *(not suitable for stock)*.
       Approximate hiking time: 1 to 1.5 hours to the lower lake, and 3 to 4 hours to the upper lake.

The 2-mile trip to the lower lake is up a rather steep forest

MAP 2 7

trail and should be taken at a fairly easy pace, especially if one is not a seasoned hiker. Lower Lena Lake, which is outside the park, is a fair-sized lake containing rainbow and eastern brook trout.

The trail to Upper Lena Lake follows the main fork of Lena Creek and breaks out into open meadow country near the upper lake, which contains rainbow trout. Mt. Bretherton (5960) can be reached by climbing to the ridge from the southeast end of the lake.

For those planning the ascent of The Brothers: the East Fork Lena Creek Trail, which is outside the park, starts at the lower lake and continues about 3 miles to a left fork in the creek. Follow this fork in a northwest direction (a faint trail may be found here and there along this route) and ascend the mountain on the southeast side.

Scout Lake Way Trail

0.0 mi. The northwest end of Upper Lena Lake.

2.0 Scout Lake turnoff.

3.0 Mt. Stone.

Approximate hiking time: 1 hour to Scout Lake turnoff and 1.5 hours to the base of Mt. Stone.

A short climb leads to the top of the north-south ridge leading to Mt. Stone. The way trail more or less follows this ridge to a narrow pass near the northeast side of Mt. Stone.

From the Scout Lake turnoff there is a drop to Scout Lake of 700 feet in 0.25 mile.

Dosewallips-Duckabush River

Duckabush River Road

This road leaves U.S. 101 22 miles north of Hoodsport and extends 7 miles up the Duckabush River through cutover land, ending 5 miles outside the park. Camp Collins, U.S. Forest Service campground, is located near the river 5 miles up this road and includes tables, stoves, and sanitary facilities.

Dosewallips River Road

0.0 mi.	U.S. 101, at Brinnon, Washington, 9 mi. south of Quilcene, or 26 mi. north of Hoodsport.
1.5	Lazy "C" Ranch.
11.2	Elkhorn Campground. U.S. Forest Service provides campsites and sanitary facilities.
13.8	National Park boundary.
14.2	Lake Constance Way Trail to Lake Constance and Mt. Constance.
15.4	Dosewallips automobile campground. In forest setting. Stoves, tables, and sanitary facilities.
15.5	Dosewallips Ranger Station. Information and backcountry use permits, summer.

This entrance road travels first through cutover forest and later through virgin Douglas-fir forest typical of east-side valleys. Near the end, the road goes through a narrow canyon, skirting huge cliffs of pillow lavas (quick-cooling lavas formed under water). Beautiful Dosewallips Falls can be seen in this canyon. Dosewallips automobile campground is the starting point of the main Dosewallips River-Hayden Pass Trail, from which branch trails lead into a high-country region of rare beauty.

Big Quilcene River Road

Leaves U.S. 101 2 miles west of Quilcene and continues 10 miles to the end of the road at Ten Mile in the Olympic National Forest.

Duckabush River-O'Neil Pass Trail

0.0 mi.	Duckabush River Road, at end.
4.8	National Park boundary.
9.3	Ten Mile.
14.7	Junction with La Crosse Pass Trail to La Crosse Pass (5566).
16.3	Upper Duckabush.

4. Dosewallips Cascades

16.4	Junction with North Fork Skokomish River Trail.
19.9	Junction with Hart and La Crosse Lakes Trail to Hart Lake (1.0 mi.) and Lake La Crosse (1.3 mi.).
19.9	Marmot Lake.
21.0	O'Neil Pass (5000) *(not suitable for stock)*. From the pass it is 7 mi. to Quinault River-Enchanted Valley Trail, 10.6 mi. to Enchanted Valley, and 21.5 mi. to Quinault River Road (Map 16).

After 1.5 miles through cutover land, this trail runs through Douglas-fir and western hemlock forest up to open meadow country. Except where the trail goes up over the Big Hump it follows a more or less even grade to a point about 0.75 mile beyond Upper Duckabush. Here it begins to climb to Marmot Lake, in open meadow and subalpine fir country. Continuing up the trail past the lake one soon reaches O'Neil Pass. A good route up Mt. Duckabush takes off from the meadows, crosses to the west glacier, and then follows the west ridge directly to the summit.

La Crosse Pass Trail

0.0 mi.	Duckabush River-O'Neil Pass Trail, 14.7 mi. up.
3.1	La Crosse Pass.
6.4	West Fork Dosewallips River-Anderson Pass Trail.
	Approximate hiking time: 3 to 4 hours.

This trail climbs 3.1 miles to La Crosse Pass (5566) and then drops 3.4 miles down to the West Fork of the Dosewallips River. Mt. La Crosse (6417) can be reached by leaving the trail at the pass and climbing southwest 1 mile up the ridge to a point just below the summit. From here the experienced rock climber must make his own way.

La Crosse Pass is 17.8 miles by trail from the end of the Duckabush River Road and 12.6 miles by trail from the end of the Dosewallips River Road.

Hart and La Crosse Lakes Trail

0.0 mi.	Duckabush River-O'Neil Pass Trail, 19.2 mi. up, or 3.4 mi. above the junction with North Fork Skokomish River Trail.
1.0	Hart Lake.

MAP 2 11

1.3   Lake La Crosse.
        Approximate hiking time: 0.5 hour to Hart Lake and 1
        hour to Lake LaCrosse.
    Turning right from the Duckabush River Trail, the trail
climbs 600 feet in 0.5 mile. Hart Lake lies a short distance to the
left of the main trail in typical subalpine fir and open meadow
country.

Lake Constance Way Trail

0.0 mi. Dosewallips River Road, 14.2 mi. up, near Constance
        Creek.
2.0   Lake Constance.
        Approximate hiking time: 2.5 to 3 hours.
    This is a steep, rough way trail which more or less follows
Constance Creek to Lake Constance (4750), which is almost
surrounded by high rock cliffs. The lake contains eastern brook
trout. Campers are often rewarded with the sight of white Rocky
Mountain goats on the rock cliffs near the lake. For the ascent of
Mt. Constance, go north up the valley for about 1.5 miles and
cross a small pass to ascend along the east face. From here the
experienced climber can determine the best route. The east
ridge contains the highest summit.

Muscott Basin (Wildcat Lake) Way Trail

0.0 mi. Dosewallips automobile campground.
3.5   End of trail.
        Approximate hiking time: 3 hours.
    This trip is over an interesting, although not maintained, way
trail which starts on the south bank of the Dosewallips River.
The trail goes up a steep grade through the forest on the east side
of Muscott Creek for about 1.5 miles and then crosses over to the
west side. Near the end of the trail is a good campsite in Muscott
Basin, with water near at hand. The best way to reach Wildcat
Lake is to cross the basin, follow a contour around to the east
ridge, and then work northeast along the ridge to its top. The
lake lies several hundred feet below the ridge on the north side.

Dosewallips River-Hayden Pass Trail

0.0 mi.   Dosewallips automobile campground.
1.4   Junction with West Fork Dosewallips River-Anderson Pass Trail.
1.45   Dose Forks.
2.5   Junction with Constance Pass Trail to Constance Pass (5 mi.).
5.1   Hattana Falls viewpoint.
9.2   Junction with Graywolf Pass Trail. Zigzags from Dosewallips River 3.4 mi. to the pass (6150) and 17.8 mi. to Deer Park Road (Map 3).
11.0   Bear Camp.
12.8   Dose Meadow and junction with Lost Pass-Cameron Pass Way Trail to Lost Pass (5550) (0.8 mi. from this junction); to end of Hurricane Ridge Road at Obstruction Point via Grand Pass Trail (14.6 mi. from junction) (Map 3); and to Deer Park Road via Cameron River Trail (18.6 mi. from junction) (Map 3).
15.4   Hayden Pass (5847). From here it is 8.4 mi. to Elwha River Trail and 25.5 mi. to Whiskey Bend Road (Maps 5, 6).

This trail follows the main Dosewallips River valley through virgin Douglas-fir and western hemlock forest before breaking out into high-country meadows a short distance below Graywolf Pass Trail junction.

From Dose Meadow, interesting one-day climbs can be made to Wellesley Peak (6758) and Lost Peak (6515) (Map 3). To reach Wellesley Peak, hike east over open meadow alpine fir and heather slopes, holding a course to the left of a low buttress for approximately 2.5 miles. Experience should point the route from here to the summit. To reach Lost Peak, take Lost Pass Way Trail to the top of the pass (5550) and then climb east on easy talus slopes (Map 3).

It is a steady 2.6 mile climb from the meadows to the top of Hayden Pass. Mt. Fromme (6655), Mt. Claywood (6836), and Sentinel Peak (6592) can be reached from the pass. The first 2 peaks lie to the northwest and can be reached by climbing a gentle ridge to the summit of Mt. Fromme, then dropping down

MAP 2   13

the east side to a small lake between the 2 summits and climbing up a talus shoulder to the higher summit of Mt. Claywood. Sentinel Peak is reached by climbing south from the pass up an easy ridge. From the summit you get a magnificent view of Eel and other glaciers on the north slopes of Mt. Anderson. Mt. Anderson, 4 to 5 miles south of Hayden Pass, can be reached via Eel Glacier. From the pass climb over a high shoulder east of Sentinel Peak and then work your way along the eastern slope for approximately 3 miles to the head of Silt Creek and Eel Glacier. From here on the experienced mountaineer can make his own way.

West Fork Dosewallips River-Anderson Pass Trail

0.0 mi.	Dosewallips River-Hayden Pass Trail, 1.4 mi. from the end of the Dosewallips River Road.
2.8	Big Timber Camp.
5.3	Diamond Meadow.
7.5	Honeymoon Meadows.
7.8	Junction with La Crosse Pass Trail to La Crosse Pass (3.3 mi.) and the Duckabush River Trail (6.4 mi.).
8.4	Anderson Pass.
9.1	Anderson Pass. Junction with trail to Anderson Glacier and Mt. Anderson (0.75 mi). From this junction it is 4.8 mi. to Enchanted Valley and 15.6 mi. to Quinault River Road (Map 16).

This trail follows the west branch of the Dosewallips River through virgin Douglas-fir and western hemlock forest. Above Diamond Meadow the trail passes through meadow and subalpine fir forest to Anderson Pass (4464). Just beyond Honeymoon Meadows the La Crosse Pass Trail turns south with a steep 3.3-mile grade to La Crosse Pass (5566); another 3.1 miles down is the junction with the Duckabush River Trail.

To reach Mt. Anderson (7321) take the 0.75-mile Anderson Glacier Trail from the summit of Anderson Pass, climbing northward through steep heather meadows to Anderson Glacier. From here the experienced climber must take over for the final assault.

5. View toward the head of the Lillian River from Moose Lake-Grand Pass Trail

MAP 2 15

Constance Pass Trail

0.0 mi. Dosewallips River-Hayden Pass Trail, 2.5 mi. up.

5.0   Constance Pass (5800). From here it is 0.4 mi. to Home
Lake, 3.8 mi. to Boulder, 5.8 mi. to Camp Handy (Map
3), and 8 mi. to the junction of Dungeness River-
Constance Pass Trail with Royal Basin Trail (Map 3).

From the Dosewallips River Trail to Constance Pass is a steep
climb; the final 1.5 miles are through open meadow country. The
pass itself affords an outstanding panorama of the surrounding
mountain ridges and peaks, including Mt. Constance (7743),
Warrior Peak (7300), and Mt. Deception (7788). Rugged Mt.
Olympus (7965) and other peaks of the interior of the Peninsula
also show from this vantage point.

Home Lake, a small lake below the pass, contains eastern brook
trout.

Mt. Mystery (7631) and Little Mystery (6941) can be reached
from this trail. From a point near the pass traverse the northwest
ridge about 3 miles to Gunsight Pass (6600), which lies between
Little Mystery and Mt. Mystery. From here, fairly easy ascents
can be made to the summits of both peaks. Mt. Deception
(7788), the highest peak in the eastern Olympic ranges, can also
be reached by this route by crossing over and down on the north
side of Mt. Mystery to the head of Deception Creek.

To reach Warrior Peak, another interesting climb, continue
down from Constance Pass to a point near the park boundary,
then turn east from the trail and follow the creek bed to the
basin between the main peak of Mt. Constance and Warrior
Peak. From the basin the final route must be determined by the
experienced mountaineer.

From the park boundary to Boulder the trail skirts the sheer
rock walls on the northwest side of Warrior Peak. From Boulder
it is a steady drop down through open forest to heavier forest at
Camp Handy (Map 3). Just below Camp Handy the trail crosses
over to the west side of the Dungeness River (Map 3).

Graywolf Pass Trail

0.0 mi. Dosewallips River-Hayden Pass Trail, 9.2 mi. up.

3.4   Graywolf Pass (6150).
        Approximate hiking time: 1.5 to 2 hours.
The trail climbs up to the pass through open meadow and subalpine fir forest. It is 17.8 miles from the Dosewallips River to the end of the Deer Park Road (Map 3). From Graywolf Pass it is 4.1 mi. to Falls (Map 3), 9.5 mi. to Cameron Creek (Map 3), and 14.4 mi. to Deer Park (Map 3).

Quilcene River Trail

0.0 mi. Big Quilcene River Road at Ten Mile.
6.2   Junction with Marmot Pass Trail at Marmot Pass (6000).
         Approximate hiking time: 4 to 5 hours.
This trail follows through Douglas-fir, western hemlock forest to the last couple of miles in open meadow subalpine fir forest country. There are 2 trailside camps, one at Shelter Rock (3.5 miles) and one at Camp Mystery (5.5 miles). At Marmot Pass the trail crosses over into the Upper Dungeness River watershed, and magnificent vistas of this large alpine area come into view.

Marmot Pass Trail

0.0 mi. Quilcene River Trail at Marmot Pass.
1.5   Dungeness River-Constance Pass Trail, near Boulder.
This trail drops down through outstanding high country. The picturesque lodgepole and whitebark pines are to be found growing near the pass, while the slopes below are covered with flowers of infinite variety. Magnificent vistas extend in every direction across the rugged Upper Dungeness Basin.

Map 3

Deer Park-Graywolf River-Cameron and Grand Creeks

Dungeness Forks Road

Leaves U.S. 101 2 miles west of Blyn, Washington at Sequim Bay State Park and continues 10 miles to Dungeness Forks. About

MAP 3 17

0.5 mile beyond Dungeness Forks, take the right fork 9 miles to its end.

Deer Park Road

0.0 mi. U.S. 101, 6 mi. east of Port Angeles.

9.0 National Park boundary.

18.0 Deer Park Ranger Station. Information and backcountry use permits, summer.

18.1 Deer Park automobile campground. Water, stoves, tables, and sanitary facilities.

19.0 Blue Mountain Lookout (6007).

A standard width black-top road extends 5 miles from U.S. 101. From here, it gradually narrows down to a one-way dirt road with turnouts.

After entering Olympic National Park this road winds up the ridge, running into steep grades near its upper end.

From the lookout station on Blue Mountain, weather permitting, you can look out over Juan de Fuca Strait and see Victoria, the capital city of British Columbia, and the San Juan Islands with the Cascade Mountains in the background. In the opposite direction can be seen the rugged snow-capped peaks and ridges of the interior Olympics.

Lost Pass-Cameron Pass Way Trail *(not suitable for stock)*

0.0 mi. Dosewallips River-Hayden Pass Trail, 12.8 mi. up (Map 2).

0.8 Lost Pass (5550).

2.8 Cameron Pass (6450).
   Approximate hiking time: 2 to 2.5 hours to Cameron Pass.

This is a rather steep way trail leading up through subalpine fir forest and open meadow country to the top of Lost Pass. The route from Lost Pass to Cameron Pass is through open meadow country.

It is 15.4 miles from Cameron Pass to Deer Park Road via the Cameron Creek-Cameron Pass and Three Forks trails, and 11.8 miles from Cameron Pass to the Hurricane Ridge Road via the Moose Lake-Grand Pass Trail.

Dungeness River-Constance Pass Trail

Where the road crosses the Dungeness River, 3.5 miles above Dungeness Forks, is the junction with Gold Creek Trail at Gold Creek. From this junction it is 9.2 miles to Tubal Cain Mine and 13 miles to Marmot Pass.

0.0 mi. End of Dungeness River Road at Muller Creek.
1.0   Junction with Royal Basin Trail. From this junction it is 6 mi. to Royal Lake and 6.2 mi. to Big Rock.
3.2   Camp Handy.
6.0   Boulder and junction with Marmot Pass Trail.
7.2   National Park boundary.
9.4   Home Lake (Map 2).
9.8   Constance Pass (5800) (Map 2). From the pass it is 5 mi. to Dosewallips River Trail (Map 2) and 7.5 mi. to Dosewallips River Road (Map 2).

This trail starts in typical old-growth western hemlock-western redcedar forest. The trail follows close to the river to above Camp Handy. The trail crosses over to the east side of the Dungeness just below Camp Handy. From Camp Handy it is a steady climb of 3 miles through thinning forest to Boulder in the upper Dungeness Valley. From Boulder the trail skirts the sheer rock walls on the northwest side of Warrior Peak and leads up to Constance Pass, where a magnificent view of the surrounding ridges and peaks extends in all directions.

Royal Basin Trail

0.0 mi. Dungeness River-Constance Pass Trail, 1.0 mi. from end of road #295.
6.2   Big Rock.
         Approximate hiking time: 3 to 3.5 hours.

The trail follows the west side of Royal Valley through gradually thinning forest to about 1 mile below Royal Lake, where it breaks out into large open meadows.

Big Rock, well named, lies at the east end of a big meadow 0.3 mile to the east of Royal Lake. The overhang of Big Rock could easily shelter 50 or more people.

6. Mt. Olympus, from Deer Park-Obstruction Point Trail

The Royal Basin covers a large area of alpine meadows surrounded on 3 sides by high rock ridges.

Deer Park-Obstruction Point Trail

0.0 mi.   Deer Park Ranger Station.
5.5   Junction with Badger Valley Way Trail.
7.6   Hurricane Ridge Road at Obstruction Point.

This trail more or less follows the top of a ridge from Deer Park to Obstruction Point. It is one of the highest trails in the park and is continuously in high, open-meadow country. From Elk Mountain (6764), near Obstruction Point, there are fine views of Mt. Olympus. To the south can be seen the Grand, Cameron, and Graywolf valleys and the rugged spires of the Needles and other peaks in the Graywolf Range. To the north, the short Mt. Angeles Range can be seen across the upper Morse Creek valley.

Three Forks Trail

0.0 mi.   Deer Park, near upper campground area.
4.5   Three Forks and Grand Creek crossing.
          Approximate hiking time: 2 hours down and 4 to 6 hours up. Trail drops 3,300 feet in the 4.5 miles.

This is a steep trail though fairly heavy forest except for the upper 0.5 mile or so, which is through typical subalpine forest. There is no water on this trail except for a small stream located about 0.5 mile above the Grand Creek crossing.

Three Forks is located beside the trail near Grand Creek. Across Grand Creek and Cameron Creek, and 0.3 mile downstream on the Cameron Creek-Cameron Pass Trail, is another good campsite called the Graywolf camp. The Graywolf River-Graywolf Pass Trail can be found just across the river from the shelter.

Slab Camp Trail

0.0 mi.   0.25 mi. east of Deer Park campground on Three Forks Trail.

MAP 3   **21**

4.75   Slab Camp Road and Slab Camp.
         Approximate hiking time: 2.5 to 3 hours.
   This trail leaves the upper campground area and continues for
a mile through open meadows; after 1.4 miles it drops down
through light forest to the park boundary. From the park
boundary to Slab Camp Road, the trail is not maintained.

Cameron Creek-Cameron Pass Trail

0.0 mi. Junction with Graywolf River-Graywolf Pass Trail.
0.1   Graywolf camp.
0.4   Junction with Three Forks Trail to Deer Park.
5.3   Lower Cameron.
7.6   Junction with Moose Lake-Grand Pass Trail.
10.0   Upper Cameron.
11.3   Cameron Pass (6450) *(not suitable for stock)*. From the
         pass it is 2.8 mi. to Dose Meadow and 15.6 mi. to Dose-
         wallips River Road (Map 2).
   This trail begins near the fork of Cameron Creek with the
Graywolf River. It continues on the south side of Cameron
Creek for over 0.5 mile and then swings over to the north side.
About a mile beyond this point it crosses over again for 0.75 mile
and then swings back, staying on the northwest side to the upper
basin. Shortly beyond Lower Cameron, the western hemlock
type of forest begins to thin out and open meadow subalpine fir
forest takes its place. The Cameron glaciers can be seen to the
southeast from near the Moose Lake-Grand Pass Trail junction.
From the upper shelter the trail begins its final climb to Cameron Pass; from the pass can be seen an excellent panorama of
the surrounding snow-capped ridges and peaks.

Graywolf River-Graywolf Pass Trail

0.0 mi. Junction with Cameron Creek-Cameron Pass Trail, across
         the river from Graywolf camp.
2.7   Camp Ellis.
5.4   Falls. Junction with Cedar Lake Way Trail to Cedar
         Lake (3.0 mi.).
9.5   Graywolf Pass (6150). From here it is 3.4 mi. to Dose-
         wallips River Trail and 12.7 mi. to Dosewallips River
         Road (Map 2).

From its junction with the Cameron Creek-Cameron Pass Trail, it follows along the east side of the Graywolf River valley for over a mile before crossing to the west side where it stays until shortly after leaving Falls. From here on, it crosses back and forth on the upper Graywolf. Above Falls the forest begins to open into meadow. The trail starts its climb to the pass a short distance beyond the falls.

The route often taken to reach the Needles leaves the trail about 1 mile beyond Falls and follows up the stream valley to the east. To reach Mt. Deception from the Graywolf, follow up the second stream valley to the east after leaving Falls.

Cedar Lake Way Trail

0.0 mi. Falls on Graywolf River-Graywolf Pass Trail, 5.4 mi. above Graywolf camp.

3.0   Cedar Lake.

This unmaintained way trail can be found by walking about 600 feet back of the falls and turning south. It climbs steeply up through the forest after leaving the open meadow. About 1 mile above the falls it emerges into a large open meadow, where it can easily be lost. Go to the south end of the meadow and look to the east across Cedar Creek to pick it up again in the forest.

Moose Lake-Grand Pass Trail

0.0 mi. End of Hurricane Ridge Road at Obstruction Point.

3.5   Junction with Badger Valley Way Trail and Grand Lake Trail, 0.3 mi. to Grand Lake.

4.1   Moose Lake.

4.7   Gladys Lake.

6.0   Grand Pass (6450) *(not suitable for stock)*. From here it is 1.9 mi. to Cameron Creek-Cameron Pass Trail.

This trail follows a north-south shale ridge for about a mile. It then turns east and descends on a rather steep grade to the Grand valley. Grand Lake is located 0.3 mile below the junction of the Moose Lake-Grand Pass Trail and Badger Valley Way Trail. Moose Lake is almost a mile from Grand Lake. From

MAP 4   **23**

Gladys Lake to the pass is a steep climb for over a mile. From the pass to the Cameron River the trail drops 2400 feet in less than 2 miles.

Badger Valley Way Trail

0.0 mi. Moose Lake-Grand Pass Trail, 3.5 mi. from Obstruction Point.

4.8   Deer Park-Obstruction Point Trail near Elk Mountain. Approximate hiking time: 2.5 to 3 hours.

This trail makes a good alternate return route back to Obstruction Point. It follows down the Grand Valley about 2 miles before turning west up Badger Valley and continuing to a junction with the Deer Park-Obstruction Point Trail. From the junction it is 2.1 miles west to the end of the Hurricane Ridge-Obstruction Point Road and 5.5 miles east to the Deer Park Ranger Station.

Heart o' the Hills-Hurricane Ridge

Heart o' the Hills Road to Hurricane Ridge

0.0 mi. At First and Race Streets on U.S. 101, 0.8 mi. inside the eastern city limits of Port Angeles.

0.8   Park Avenue. Olympic National Park Headquarters are 0.5 mi. to the west.

1.0   Olympic National Park Port Angeles Visitor Center. Information and exhibits on Olympic National Park. Backcountry use permits.

5.3   National Park boundary.

5.7   Elwha River Road 8 mi. from here via Little River Road.

5.8   Heart o' the Hills Ranger Station. Road to Lake Angeles and Mt. Angeles trailheads.

5.9   Heart o' the Hills Campground.

7. Looking north from Hurricane Hill, with view of Port Angeles, Ediz Hook, Juan de Fuca Strait, Vancouver Island, and the San Juan Islands

MAP 4 25

6.1   Lake Creek Trail. 4 mi. to Mt. Pleasant Road.
9.4   Lookout point. View point and parking area.
17.8   Junction with alpine drive. 8.4 mi. to Obstruction Point.
18.0   Hurricane Ridge Lodge.

This road is the entrance way to the Heart o' the Hills-Hurricane Ridge area. Olympic National Park Headquarters and Museum are located near the road.

Heart o' the Hills is situated at the base of the Mt. Angeles Range directly south of Port Angeles. Several excellent trails lead from here to interesting high-country areas, including Lake Angeles. The nearness to Port Angeles makes this area ideal for one-day trips.

Hurricane Ridge Lodge, located in Big Meadow, provides a sweeping view of the high, mountainous interior of the park. The lodge provides lunch counter service.

Hurricane Hill Approach Road

0.0 mi.   Hurricane Ridge Lodge.
1.0   Hurricane Hill picnic area, tables, water, and sanitary facilities.
1.3   End of road.
1.5   Start of Little River Trail to Little River Road at Shore Ranch (8.1 mi.).
2.7   Hurricane Hill (5757).

This mile-high road approaches Hurricane Hill, which is at the western end of Hurricane Ridge. Starting from the parking area at the end of the road, a paved trail with interpretive signs leads to the top of Hurricane Hill. Trailside exhibits explain features seen along the 1.4 mile walk. Outstanding views of the interior of the park can be seen from here.

Hurricane Ridge-Obstruction Point Road *(steep and narrow, not paved)*

0.0 mi.   Junction with Heart o' the Hills Road at Big Meadow.
0.4   Start of Cox Valley Way Trail.

1.1   Steeple Rock (5567).
3.9   Waterhole.
4.9   Eagle Point (6247).
8.4   Obstruction Point. End of Hurricane Ridge Road. Start
         of Moose Lake-Grand Pass Trail (Map 3).

This is a high ridge road following the crest from Hurricane
Ridge Lodge (5225) to its end near Obstruction Peak (6450).
Beautiful fields of alpine flowers cover the meadows during July
and August. In the early mornings and late evenings deer can be
seen feeding in the meadows. Often during the day the western
redtailed hawk, singly or in pairs, can be watched soaring on the
strong mountain air currents. As the road passes beyond the
obstructing ridges Mt. Olympus looms bigger and bigger on the
western skyline.

From the end of the Hurricane Ridge Road a trail leads along
the ridge to Deer Park, 7.6 miles away (Map 3).

Lake Angeles Trail

0.0 mi. Near Heart o' the Hills Ranger Station.
3.5   Lake Angeles.
         Approximate hiking time: 1.5 to 2 hours.

This trail climbs through old, second-growth Douglas-fir and
western hemlock forest for the first 2.5 miles. From here on the
forest gradually changes to subalpine fir and hemlock and begins
to thin out, affording excellent views of Klahhane Rock to the
east.

Lake Angeles, one of the largest subalpine lakes in Olympic
National Park, is enclosed on 3 sides by high cliffs forming a
huge cirque. Mountain goats are often seen on the rocks near and
above the lake.

Klahhane Ridge Trail

0.0 mi. Lake Angeles trail near Lake Angeles.
3.0   Mt. Angeles-Big Meadow Trail along Klahhane Ridge.
         Approximate hiking time: 2 to 3 hours.

MAP 4 27

The trail climbs very steeply up the east side of Ennis Ridge and then swings over to the west side above the headwaters of Ennis Valley. Following this side for 0.5 mile it climbs over the top of the ridge to the east side again above Lake Angeles. From here it climbs up to Klahhane Ridge, which it follows west to the Mt. Angeles-Big Meadow Trail. From this high ridge marvelous panoramas extend both north and south.

Mt. Angeles-Big Meadow Trail

0.0 mi.	Heart o' the Hills Ranger Station.
2.2	Halfway Rock lookout point.
4.1	Heather Park.
4.6	Heather Pass. Junction with way trails to First and Second Peak summits.
6.4	Klahhane Ridge summit (5850). Junction with Klahhane Ridge Trail. From here it is 3 mi. to Lake Angeles.
7.9	Junction with way trail to summit of Mt. Angeles (6454).
10.0	Big Meadow and Hurricane Ridge Lodge.

The trail follows through second-growth Douglas-fir and western hemlock forest to a point a short distance above Halfway Rock. Here the forest begins to thin out, allowing excellent views out over Juan de Fuca Strait to the shores and mountains of Vancouver Island, and over the country east of Port Angeles.

Heather Park lies like a small gem encased by the rocky ridges of First Peak and Second Peak. The flower display in this small alpine park is usually a beautiful sight during July.

From Heather Pass it is only a short climb to the top of First Peak (5510). The climbing of Second Peak (6039) requires some moderate rock work and should not be attempted by inexperienced climbers.

The main trail continues up and down through several rock screes and meadows, finally reaching the summit of Klahhane Ridge (5850) at the head of Ennis Creek basin. The experienced mountaineer can find routes of varying degrees of difficulty to the top of Mt. Angeles (6454) to the west. To the east, Klahhane Ridge Trail and Lake Angeles Trail lead, in 6.5 miles, to Heart o' the Hills. A way trail to Mt. Angeles leaves the main trail 1.5 miles below Klahhane Ridge.

Toward Big Meadow, the trail drops down fast to a south ridge, which it follows to Hurricane Ridge.

Lake Creek Trail

0.0 mi. Heart o' the Hills Campground.
4.0　　Mt. Pleasant Road at Hambly Ranch.
　　　　Approximate hiking time: 1.5 to 2 hours.

This trail traverses fairly level country. Some of the finest stands of old-growth virgin Douglas-fir and western redcedar can be seen near the trail. The last mile of this trail follows above Lake Creek through more or less cutover forest. The trail connects the Heart o' the Hills Road with the Mt. Pleasant Road.

Little River Trail

0.0 mi. Hurricane Hill Trail, 1.5 mi. from Hurricane Ridge Lodge.
8.1　　Little River Road near the Shore Ranch.
　　　　Approximate hiking time: 3 to 4 hours.

The upper reaches of this trail alternate through meadow and subalpine fir forest; it then follows, through dense forest, first one side and then the other side of the stream. The plant cover under old-growth forest in the lower valley is particularly luxuriant.

Cox Valley Way Trail

0.0 mi. Hurricane Ridge Road, 0.4 mi. from Big Meadow.
1.7　　Cox Valley (old log cabin).
　　　　Approximate hiking time: 1 hour down and 2 hours up.

This trail goes first through subalpine fir forest and then through alternating meadow and forest. The large meadows are luxuriant and full of colorful flowers in July and August.

8. The short cut trail from the Hurricane Ridge Road to the
Klahhane Ridge Trail is a good way to hike to
Lake Angeles or Heather Park.

Map 5

Lower Elwha River-Boulder Creek

Elwha River-Boulder Creek Road

0.0 mi.   U.S. 101, 9 mi. west of Port Angeles.

2.0   National Park boundary.

3.0   Elwha Campground. Stoves, tables, sanitary facilities located in cottonwood and alder bottom forest setting. Starting point of Cascade Rock Way Trail.

4.0   Elwha Ranger Station. Information and backcountry use permits. Starting point of Griff Creek Trail.

4.1   Junction with road to Whiskey Bend (5 mi.).

4.2   Altaire Campground. Stoves, tables, sanitary facilities; in cottonwood and alder bottom forest setting along west bank of Elwha River. Start of West Elwha Trail.

5.4   Glines Canyon Dam and Lake Mills. Start of Lake Mills Trail.

7.9   Observation Point. An excellent view up the Elwha Valley.

8.7   Happy Lake Ridge Trail. Leads to Happy Lake and high open country above Boulder Creek Canyon.

11.7   Boulder Creek Campground. Stoves, tables, restrooms; located in forest of old-growth Douglas-fir and western redcedar.

This improved road follows the east side of the Elwha River valley to Altaire Campground, where it crosses the river and starts to climb to Boulder Creek.

In the late winter and early spring white Rocky Mountain goats can often be seen on the massive lava rock outcroppings on

MAP 5 31

the west side of the valley. Roosevelt elk can frequently be seen in the maple-alder-cottonwood bottoms along the Elwha River.

The Elwha and Altaire campgrounds are both situated in attractive forest settings of maple, alder, and cottonwood.

Soon after crossing the Elwha River near Altaire Campground, the road affords a view of Lake Mills with snow-capped Mt. Fitzhenry in the background. Near Observation Point, a wide panorama opens up over the upper and lower Elwha valleys. In this vicinity the Pacific madrone, or madrona, a reddish-orange, smooth-barked tree, will be found growing. From this point the road runs above the deep, dark canyon of Boulder Creek.

Whiskey Bend Road

0.0 mi. Junction with Elwha River-Boulder Creek Road, 4.1 mi.
       from U.S. 101.
4.5 Upper Lake Mills Trail.
5.0 Whiskey Bend. Start of Elwha River Trail.

Cascade Rock Way Trail

0.0 mi. Elwha Campground, across small creek near community
       kitchen.
2.0 Cascade Rock.
       Approximate hiking time: 1.5 to 2 hours.

This trail climbs steadily on a spur ridge leading to the Elwha River Range. It is in the forest all the way to the rock.

A portion of the Elwha River, Glines Canyon Dam, and Lake Mills can be seen from the top.

Griff Creek Trail

0.0 mi. Start back of Elwha Ranger Station.
2.8 End of the trail.
       Approximate hiking time: 1.5 to 2 hours.

After following up Griff Creek a short distance this trail turns to the left and leads, by switchbacks, up a spur ridge of the Elwha River Range to a dead end in the rocks.

West Elwha Trail

0.0 mi. Altaire Campground, near community kitchen.
2.6   National Park boundary.
         Approximate hiking time: 1.5 to 2 hours.
This trail goes along the west bank of the Elwha River to the park boundary near the end of the West Elwha River Road. In the winter months small bands of elk can sometimes be seen from this trail.

As it approaches the park boundary the trail passes through a typical old-growth Douglas-fir and western hemlock forest with its luxuriant undergrowth of shade-loving plants.

Lake Mills Trail

0.0 mi. Elwha River-Boulder Creek Road, near Glines Canyon Dam.
2.0   Boulder Creek.
         Approximate hiking time: 1 to 1.5 hours.
This trail follows the west side of Lake Mills and ends at Boulder Creek. This is an excellent early spring and summer hiking trail. Since it follows close to the shoreline, it is fairly level.

Happy Lake Ridge Trail

0.0 mi. Elwha River-Boulder Creek Road, 8.7 mi. from U.S. 101.
4.5   Happy Lake Trail junction, 0.5 mi. to the the lake.
7.0   Aurora Divide Trail junction. From here it is 17.2 mi. to the Upper Soleduck River-Hot Springs Road and 9.8 mi. to Lake Crescent Lodge (Map 7).
9.7   Boulder Lake. From here it is 3.4 mi. to Boulder Creek Campground.
This trail climbs up to the top of Happy Lake Ridge through forest which opens out into wide meadow areas where thrilling

MAP 5 **33**

views may be had of Juan de Fuca Strait and of the rugged interior mountains of Olympic National Park.

White Rocky Mountain goats are often seen on the rocks above Happy Lake. The lake contains eastern brook trout.

Appleton Pass Trail

0.0 mi. Boulder Creek Campground.
0.6   Junction with Boulder Lake Trail to Boulder Lake and connection with Happy Lake Ridge Trail (2.8 mi.).
5.2   Appleton Pass (5000).
7.8   Junction with Soleduck River Trail to High Divide (Maps 7, 12). From here it is 2.8 mi. to Soleduck Park and 4.9 mi. to Soleduck River Road.

The first 4.5 miles lead through old-growth Douglas-fir forest before breaking out into open meadow areas. From the divide an interesting view can be seen of glacier-clad Mt. Olympus to the south of High Divide. Toward the east, past small Oyster Lake, fields of mountain flowers bloom during the summer.

Boulder Lake Trail

0.0 mi. Appleton Pass Trail, 0.6 mi. from Boulder Creek Campground.
2.8   Boulder Lake.

Hurricane Hill Trail

0.0 mi. 0.1 mi. from junction of Whiskey Bend Road with Elwha River-Boulder Creek Road.
6.0   Lookout Point (5757).
       Approximate hiking time: 3 to 4 hours.

From the starting point this trail climbs steadily up through heavy old-growth Douglas-fir and western hemlock forest to the open meadows near the top of Hurricane Hill.

Upper Lake Mills Trail *(not suitable for stock)*

0.0 mi. Whiskey Bend Road, 4.5 mi. up.
0.4   Lake Mills.
       Approximate hiking time: 15 to 20 minutes down and 30 to 40 minutes up.

9. Blizzard Pass, from Blue Glacier

MAP 5 35

This trail drops steeply from the road to the shores of Lake Mills, where camping is permitted.

Elwha River Trail

0.0 mi.	Whiskey Bend. Parking area.
1.5	Junction with Krause Bottom Trail. 0.5 mi. down to the flats along the Elwha River.
1.8	Junction with Long Ridge Trail to Dodger Point (11.7 mi.) and to a dead end near Ludden Peak (12.3 mi.).
4.1	Junction with Lillian River Trail, which comes to a dead end approximately 3.5 mi. up the river.
4.7	Lillian.
8.8	Marys Falls Camp.
10.5	Canyon Camp.
11.5	Elkhorn Guard Station.
11.7	Stony Point Camp.
13.0	Junction with Dodger Point Way Trail. 5.7 mi. to Dodger Point.
15.9	Tipperary Camp (Map 6).
16.8	Hayes River Guard Station (Map 6).
17.0	Junction with Hayden Pass Trail (Map 6). 8.4 mi. to Hayden Pass and 23.8 mi. to the Dosewallips River Road (Map 2).
20.9	Camp Wilder (Map 6).
25.8	Chicago Camp (Map 6). Junction with Low Divide Trail. From this junction it is 2.6 mi. to Low Divide and 19 mi. to the North Fork Quinault River Road (Map 15).
27.0	Happy Hollow on Elwha Basin Trail.
28.8	Elwha Basin Camp (Map 6). End of Elwha River Trail.

This trail, affording good river fishing, starts at Whiskey Bend, which is 9 miles from U.S. 101. It follows a more or less easy grade, except where it dips down into the Lillian valley and out again. From Dorothy Creek on, it follows fairly close to the river. It continues through typical Douglas-fir and western hemlock forest to near its upper end.

The Elwha Basin is a starting point for the following climbs: Mt. Olympus via Dodwell-Rixon Pass, Queets Basin, Humes Glacier, Mt. Meany, Mt. Queets, Mt. Seattle, and Mt. Barnes. To reach the upper snow-finger from the end of the main Elwha

Trail, keep to the left, or southwest, over a brush way trail above the rocks. Once on the upper snow-finger, it is an easy walk to the Dodwell-Rixon Pass (5000).

Krause Bottom Trail

0.0 mi.   Elwha River Trail, 1.5 mi. from Whiskey Bend.
0.5   Krause Bottom.
1.0   Humes Ranch.
1.3   Junction with Long Ridge Trail.
            Approximate hiking time: 1 to 1.5 hours from Whiskey Bend.

Krause Bottom makes a good starting point for up-river fishing. It is also an excellent area, in late April or May, for observation of spring migrating elk. Bands of these magnificent animals sometimes stay for several weeks in this area before continuing on their way to summer grazing grounds in the high country.

Long Ridge Trail

0.0 mi.   Elwha River Trail, 1.8 mi. from Whiskey Bend.
0.2   Junction with Krause Bottom Trail to Humes Ranch (0.2 mi.).
1.3   Junction with Anderson Ranch Trail to Anderson Ranch (2 mi.).
11.2   Junction with spur trail to Dodger Point Lookout (5.5 mi.).
11.7   Termination of Long Ridge Trail. Dodger Point Way Trail continues 4.7 mi. to Elwha River Trail. Way trail to Ludden Peak.
13.2   Way trail comes to dead end on the south side of Ludden Peak. Start of cross-country trip to Mt. Ferry in Bailey Range. (Rough route, not maintained.)

For the first 2 miles the trail descends to the Elwha River. Soon after crossing the bridge it starts the climb up Long Ridge by a series of switchbacks. It is a long, dry climb up to Dodger Point, as there is no water on this trail. The average hiker, with pack and in a good physical condition, would find the trip to Dodger Point a full day's journey.

MAP 5   **37**

Anderson Ranch Trail

0.0 mi. Long Ridge Trail, 1.3 mi. above Elwha River Trail.
2.0   Anderson Ranch.
           Approximate hiking time: 2.5 hours from Whiskey Bend.

Immediately after the crossing of the Elwha River, the trail branches to the right, down the west side of the river. It crosses Long Creek and meanders through typical river-bottom forests of red alder and black cottonwood to the site of the old Anderson Ranch, where the Elwha River enters Rica Canyon through Goblin Gate.

Lillian River Trail

0.0 mi. Elwha River Trail, 4.1 mi. from Whiskey Bend.
2.5   End of the trail.
           Approximate hiking time: 1.5 hours from the Elwha River Trail.

For the first 2.5 miles the trail contours around the side of the ridge some distance above the Lillian River. It then starts to drop down to the river, where it ends. A short distance above the trail's end the river runs through a deep canyon.

Dodger Point Way Trail *(not suitable for stock)*

0.0 mi. Elwha River Trail, 13 mi. from Whiskey Bend.
4.7   Long Ridge Trail.
           Approximate hiking time: 3 to 4 hours.

The point of crossing of the Elwha River varies because of the frequent floods sweeping the temporary bridges away. Check with the park ranger beforehand. This is a steep winding trail through forest, until it emerges into open meadows near the top of the ridge.

Map 6

Upper Elwha River

Elwha River Trail

See discussion under Map 5.

Hayden Pass Trail

0.0 mi. Elwha River Trail, 17.0 mi. from Whiskey Bend.
8.4   Hayden Pass (5847).
         Approximate hiking time: 4 to 5 hours.
   The lower half of this trail is in the forest, and the upper half
is through open meadows. It climbs quite steadily from the
Elwha River to the pass.

Low Divide Trail

0.0 mi. Elwha River Trail, 24.8 mi. from Whiskey Bend.
2.6   Low Divide. From Low Divide it is 16.4 mi. to the North
         Fork Quinault River Road (Map 15).
         Approximate hiking time: 2 to 3 hours.
   Soon after crossing the Elwha River the trail starts a steep
climb up to Low Divide (3600). Lake Mary, containing eastern
brook trout, and Lake Margaret are in forest settings near the
summit. Two-tenths of a mile southeast of Low Divide the
Skyline Trail leads off to the east (Map 15).

Martins Park Way Trail *(not suitable for stock)*

0.0 mi. Near Low Divide on east end of Lake Margaret.
1.0   Martins Park.
2.3   Martins Lakes.

10. Bogachiel River valley. Dense forests cover the Olympics
up to 5,000 feet

Approximate hiking time: 1 hour to Martins Park and 1.5 hours to the lakes.

The first part of the trail to Martins Park goes through a rather swampy area, but once past this the trail hits firmer ground. Mt. Seattle and the upper Elwha River Basin can be seen through the trees. The park is a large meadow area surrounded by snow fields and high rock walls. Many huge glacial boulders among fields of heather and mountain huckleberry give it a wildness of unsurpassed beauty.

The 2 Martins Lakes lie on a high bench above the park. Neither lake contains trout.

Map 7

Lake Crescent-Upper Soleduck River

East Beach-Piedmont Road

0.0 mi.   U.S. 101, 17 mi. west of Port Angeles.
0.7   National Park boundary.
3.1   Piedmont. Lake Crescent Log Cabin Lodge. Cabins, trailer space, grocery store, and boats.
3.2   Boundary Creek Forest Road to State 112.
3.6   National Park boundary.
7.5   State 112.

About 1 mile from U.S. 101 this road affords a view of Lake Crescent, and it follows the shore of the lake to Piedmont, where it turns north to Joyce.

Lake Crescent Log Cabin Lodge has housekeeping cabins, boat rentals, groceries, and trailer space with electricity and water.

MAP 7   41

Boundary Creek Forest Road

0.0 mi. 3.2 mi. from U.S. 101 on East Beach-Piedmont Road.
0.7   Lyre River.
1.2   National Park boundary.
4.0   State 112.

This one-way dirt road crosses the Lyre River and continues through State Forest land to State 112 near Deep Creek.

U.S. 101

0.0 mi. National Park boundary, 17.9 mi. west of Port Angeles.
3.1   Storm King Visitor Center. Nature Trail, Barnes Creek Trail. Mt. Storm King Way Trail, Marymere Falls Nature Trail.
3.5   Lake Crescent Ranger Station. Backcountry use permits and information.
3.6   Lake Crescent Lodge. Lodge rooms, cabins, dining room, cocktail lounge, and boats.
6.1   Aurora Creek Way Trail. From here it is 3.5 mi. to Aurora Ridge Trail.
7.6   Lapoel picnic area.
10.6   Junction with North Shore Lake Crescent Road. Fairholm Campground, modern comfort stations, campfire circle, and boat-launching ramp.
12.2   Junction with Upper Soleduck River-Hot Springs Road, which is 14 mi. long.

The highway follows the south shore of Lake Crescent, which is the largest lake in the park and an outstanding attraction. The lake is surrounded by high forested mountains, and the ever-changing blue-green of its deep waters against the background of conifer-clad slopes makes a picture not easily forgotten.

The Storm King Visitor Center located at the foot of rugged Mt. Storm King is close to Lake Crescent Lodge. This lodge is pleasantly situated, away from the main highway, in a forested area on the lake shore. It offers hotel rooms and cabins with or without housekeeping. Lake Crescent Lodge has complete dining room service. Rowboats are free to guests of the lodge.

For those wishing to rough it, the National Park Service maintains a campground at Fairholm. Also at this end of the lake are a grocery store, gasoline station, and housekeeping cabins.

North Shore Lake Crescent Road

0.0 mi. Junction with U.S. 101 near west end of Lake Crescent.
3.5   Pyramid Peak Trail. It is 3.5 mi. to Pyramid Peak.
5.0   End of the road.

This narrow road follows the north side of Lake Crescent, affording many excellent vistas across the lake.

Upper Soleduck River-Hot Springs Road

0.0 mi. Junction with U.S. 101, 30 mi. west of Port Angeles.
2.5   Aurora Ridge Trail. From here it is 15.5 mi. to Aurora Divide Trail and 17.3 mi. to Happy Lake Ridge Trail.
8.5   North Fork Soleduck Trail to end of trail (9.0 mi.).
12.3   Soleduck Ranger Station. Backcountry use permits and information.
12.5   Sol Duc Hot Springs Resort.
12.5   Mink Lake and Lovers' Lane trails.
12.8   Soleduck Campground. Individual campsites with water, stoves, tables, and comfort stations.
14.2   End of the road and start of Soleduck River Trail.

The first few miles of this road are through logged-off hills, then through old-growth Douglas-fir and western hemlock. The Soleduck River is one of the longest on the Olympic Peninsula. The upper Soleduck River is a favorite fishing area of many anglers.

The resort offers housekeeping cabins, a lunchroom, a grocery store, and a large swimming pool.

From the end of this road forest trails lead into a high country of exceptional beauty.

11. Soleduck Falls

Marymere Falls Nature Trail

0.0 mi. Storm King Visitor Center.
1.4   Round trip.

Guide booklets are available at the beginning of the trail. This self-guiding trail will help you to understand the forest and to know its trees and smaller plants. The trail leads to 90-foot Marymere Falls.

Barnes Creek Trail

0.0 mi. U.S. 101 near Storm King Visitor Center.
0.4   Junction with Mt. Storm King Way Trail.
0.5   Junction with Marymere Falls Trail. From this junction it is 0.2 mi. to the falls.
3.9   Junction with Aurora Divide Trail. From this junction it is 11.4 mi. to Boulder Creek via Aurora Divide, Happy Lake Ridge, and Boulder Lake trails (Map 5).
9.1   Junction with Lookout Dome Way Trail. From here it is 0.3 mi. to Lookout Dome.
9.2   End of trail on Barnes-Hughes Creek Divide.

Leading back through a fine old-growth forest of Douglas-fir, western hemlock, and redcedar, the trail follows the east side of Barnes Creek for over a mile and then crosses over to the west side where it continues to its end on top of the Barnes-Hughes Creek Divide. This trail is in the forest continuously from start to finish.

Mt. Storm King Way Trail *(not suitable for stock)*

0.0 mi. Storm King Visitor Center.
2.1   Top of the ridge.
         Approximate hiking time: 2 to 2.5 hours.

This trail makes a stiff climb to a point halfway to the top of Mt. Storm King. Only the experienced mountaineer should continue beyond this point. From the upper section of the trail the clear blue waters of Lake Crescent can be seen. At the highest point on the trail the view includes Juan de Fuca Strait and Vancouver Island, as well as Mt. Olympus and other peaks of the

MAP 7   **45**

interior Olympics. The Rocky Mountain goat can sometimes be observed here in his natural habitat.

Aurora Divide Trail

0.0 mi.   3.9 mi. from U.S. 101, via Barnes Creek Trail.

3.6   Junction with Aurora Ridge Trail. From this junction it is 15.5 mi. to the Upper Soleduck River-Hot Springs Road.

5.5   Junction with Happy Lake Ridge Trail. From here it is 5.9 mi. to Boulder Creek via Happy Lake Ridge and Boulder Lake trails.

A series of switchbacks climbs to the top of the divide between Barnes Creek and the North Fork of the Soleduck River. From here the trail follows the top of the ridge 1.8 miles to Happy Lake Ridge. It is 15.3 miles from Lake Crescent to Boulder Creek via the following trails: Barnes Creek, Aurora Divide, Happy Lake Ridge, and Boulder Lake.

Aurora Creek Way Trail *(not suitable for stock)*

0.0 mi. U.S. 101, 3.0 mi. west of the Storm King Visitor Center.

3.5   Aurora Ridge Trail.
       Approximate hiking time: 2 to 3 hours.

This is a very steep trail leading up to the Aurora Ridge Trail. Although forest extends to the top of the ridge, there are some excellent vistas of Lake Crescent near the top.

Pyramid Peak Trail

0.0 mi. North Shore Lake Crescent Road, 3.5 mi. from U.S. 101.

3.5   Summit of Pyramid Peak (3100).
       Approximate hiking time: 2 to 2.5 hours.

As you climb up this trail you can enjoy the ever-changing vistas over the blue-green waters of Lake Crescent. At the summit is a World War II aircraft spotters' station.

Aurora Ridge Trail

0.0 mi. Upper Soleduck River-Hot Springs Road, 2.5 mi. from U.S. 101.

6.2   Eagle Lake. This small lake contains eastern brook trout.

8.5   Sourdough camp.

10.6   Junction with Aurora Creek Way Trail to Lake Crescent (3.5 mi.).

15.5   End of Aurora Ridge Trail and junction with Aurora Divide Trail. From this junction it is 7.6 mi. to U.S. 101 and Lake Crescent and 7.7 mi. to Boulder Creek.

The first 1.5 miles of this trail are a steep climb to the top of the ridge. From here on to Happy Lake Ridge the trail runs up and down along the top of the ridge. Although the forests extend to the top of ridge, openings afford excellent views both to the interior of the park and across Lake Crescent.

North Fork Soleduck Trail

0.0 mi. Upper Soleduck River-Hot Springs Road, 8.5 mi. up.

9.0   End of trail.
         Approximate hiking time: 4 to 5 hours.

The trail climbs 1 mile over a ridge into the North Fork Soleduck River valley, continues another 6 miles on the north side of the river, and then crosses back to the south side. The route is through Douglas-fir and western hemlock forest. Fishing is very popular along this fork of the Soleduck River.

Mink Lake-Little Divide Trail

0.0 mi. Sol Duc Hot Springs Resort

4.3   Bogachiel River Trail on the divide.
         Approximate hiking time: 2.5 to 3 hours.

It is a pleasant hike to Mink Lake, 2.5 miles from the hot springs resort.

MAP 7 47

Lovers' Lane Trail

0.0 mi. Sol Duc Hot Springs Resort.
2.8   Deer Lake-Bogachiel Peak Trail.
         Approximate hiking time: 1.5 hours.

This is a hike up the west side of the Soleduck River to the Deer Lake-Bogachiel Peak Trail. By crossing the river at Soleduck Falls the hiker can return to the hot springs on the Soleduck River Trail and the road. The 5-mile round trip past the falls takes approximately 3 hours.

Soleduck River-High Divide Trail

0.0 mi. End of Upper Soleduck River-Hot Springs Road, 14.2 mi. from U.S. 101.
0.9   Junction with Deer Lake-Bogachiel Peak Trail. 7.7 mi. to Bogachiel Peak.
0.9   Soleduck Falls.
4.9   Junction with Appleton Pass Trail. From here it is 2.6 mi. to the pass and 7.8 mi. to Boulder Creek·(Map 5).
5.4   Upper Soleduck.
7.7   Soleduck Park.
8.1   Heart Lake.
8.5   Junction with High Divide Trail. From here the Upper Soleduck River Road is 10.4 mi. on the High Divide and Deer Lake-Bogachiel Peak trails.

A few miles up this trail is an almost pure stand of old-growth western hemlock with some Douglas-fir, the best example of original forest found on the east and north sides of the park. This kind of forest continues to about 1 mile below Soleduck Park.

At Soleduck Falls the river flows swiftly through a steep-sided, narrow canyon. There are several low falls on the upper Soleduck where the river has cut deep canyons.

Soon after crossing the Soleduck River the trail climbs steeply up to Soleduck Park. This park is in beautiful open meadow country. From here on to Heart Lake and the High Divide the trail continues through open meadow country.

12. High Divide Trail

MAP 7 49

Deer Lake-Bogachiel Peak Trail

0.0 mi. Soleduck Falls, 1 mi. above the end of the Upper Soleduck River-Hot Springs Road.

3.0 Deer Lake.

3.1 Junction with terminus of Bogachiel River Trail. From
here it is 26.4 mi. to the park boundary at the end of the
Bogachiel River Road (Map 11).

6.5 Junction with Seven Lakes Basin Trail. 0.8 mi. to
shelters.

7.4 Junction with High Divide and Hoh Lake trails (5200).

After leaving Soleduck Falls the trail climbs steadily through
the forest, which begins to open up about a mile above Deer
Lake. After another mile it finally reaches the top of a ridge
which is the divide between the Soleduck and Upper Bogachiel
valleys. The trail soon crosses over to the Bogachiel side, where
it follows the upper Bogachiel Basin to Bogachiel Peak. The
unobstructed view from this trail across the upper Bogachiel
Basin is breath-taking. When you top the High Divide the
7965-foot Mt. Olympus bursts upon you with sudden impact.

High Divide Trail

0.0 mi. Deer Lake-Bogachiel Peak Trail, 7.4 mi. from Soleduck
Falls. Terminus of Hoh Lake Trail.

0.2 Bogachiel Peak turnoff. 0.1 mi. to Bogachiel Peak (5474).

2.1 Junction with terminus of Soleduck River-High Divide
Trail.

5.1 Trail comes to a dead end on the south side of Cat Peak
(Map 12).

From Bogachiel Peak can be seen the ocean to the far west,
the glacier-scoured Seven Lakes Basin to the north, and majestic
Mt. Olympus to the south.

Between Bogachiel Peak and Cat Creek Basin on this trail
there is a succession of breath-taking views across the upper
Hoh valley to snow-covered Mt. Olympus with its several large
glaciers.

From Cat Creek Basin to the base of Cat Peak, the trail follows
the ridge through a stand of mountain hemlock and subalpine
fir, affording a glimpse now and then of Mt. Olympus. Near

Cat Peak the trail breaks out into the open again with unobstructed views of the Bailey and Olympus mountain ranges.

Bogachiel River Trail

See discussion under Map 11.

Lake Ozette-Rialto Beach

Lake Ozette Road

0.0 mi. Junction of U.S. 101 and Burnt Mt. Road at Sappho, 45
         mi. west of Port Angeles. Turn north at this junction.
17.0   Clallam Bay
20.9   Junction of State 112 and Lake Ozette Road.
40.8   Lake Ozette Resort.
40.9   Lake Ozette Ranger Station near the end of Lake Ozette
         Road. Information and backcountry use permits.

From the end of the Lake Ozette Road, 2 trails lead to the
ocean beaches. One of these, the Indian Village Trail, leads
to the site of an abandoned Ozette Indian village.

An excellent triangular trip consists of hiking over the Indian
Village Trail to Cape Alava, then walking 3 miles south on the
beach and following the Sand Point Trail back to the starting
point.

Indian Village Trail

0.0 mi. End of Lake Ozette Road.
3.3   Cape Alava Beach.
         Approximate hiking time: 1.5 to 2 hours.

This fairly level hike leads to the beach through typical oceanside forest with aged moss-covered trees, dense underbrush, and
shoulder-high ferns. Open areas of woods, with broken treetops

MAP 8 **51**

and snags, show the havoc wrought by wild coastal storms. Ozette Island looms about a mile offshore from the beach. Nothing is visible of the old Indian village.

Sand Point Trail

0.0 mi. End of Lake Ozette Road.
3.0 Sand Point Beach.
Approximate hiking time: 1.5 to 2 hours.

This trail is similar to the Indian Village Trail. A smooth sandy beach extends southeast 1.5 miles. At an exceptionally low tide the beach may extend out almost half a mile.

The hike up the beach to Cape Alava and the Indian Village Trail includes about a mile of rough going over a jumble of rocks, which storms have torn away from the cliffs above the beach. If you observe closely you will see rocks with Indian carvings near the beach about 2 miles north of Sand Point.

Ericsons Bay Trail

0.0 mi. Ericsons Bay on west shore of Lake Ozette.
1.9 Ocean beach.
Approximate hiking time: 1 hour.

The best way to reach this trail is by boat from Lake Ozette Resort at the north end of Lake Ozette. The trail is fairly even and goes through typical oceanside forest with dense underbrush. From the point at which the trail reaches the coast, it is approximately 0.5 mile along the sandy beach to the Sand Point Trail, and 3 more miles back to the road at Lake Ozette. A boat-in campground is located at Ericsons Bay.

Allens Bay Trail

0.0 mi. Allens Bay, 7 mi. south of Lake Ozette Resort.
2.3 Norwegian Memorial and end of the trail on the beach.
Approximate hiking time: 1.5 to 2 hours.

This trail is reached by boat from Lake Ozette Resort. For the most part the trail is level. Just before reaching the beach it enters an open area. About 150 feet north of this point is the Norwegian Memorial, which commemorates the shipwreck of 18

Norwegian sailors who lost their lives on January 2, 1903, when the three-masted bark "Prince Arthur of Norway" was blown to her doom on the rock-strewn coast.

It is a 7.5-mile hike along the beach to the Sand Point Trail. Yellow Banks can be passed only at low tide.

Rialto Beach-Cape Alava Ocean Beach Way Trail

0.0 mi. Rialto Beach at end of Rialto Beach Road (Map 9).

1.5   Point No. 1. A small point which can be rounded at low tide or climbed over.

3.0   Cape Johnson. Can be rounded only at low tide.

5.0   Point No. 2. Must be climbed over but is not difficult.

6.8   Cedar Creek. Can be easily waded.

7.0   Point No. 3. Must be rounded at low tide or climbed over. A steep trail leads up the south slope to a saddle, then down the north slope. An abandoned Coast Guard cabin is located at the tip of this point.

7.5   Allens Bay Trail and Norwegian Memorial. 2.3 mi. to Allens Bay on Lake Ozette.

13.5   Point No. 4. A vertical slide area of loose material. Must be rounded at low tide.

15.0   Ericsons Bay Trail. 1.9 mi. to Ericsons Bay on Lake Ozette.

15.5   Sand Point Trail. 3 mi. to end of Lake Ozette Road.

17.0   Point No. 5. Wedding Rock. Site of Indian petroglyphs, or rock carvings. Can be crossed by a narrow strip of land behind the rocks.

18.5   Cape Alava. Junction with Indian Village Trail leading 3 mi. to end of Lake Ozette Road.

This rugged stretch of coastline consists of beaches separated by bold headlands. Thousands of people have hiked this route and found it entirely pleasurable. However, some precaution should be taken. It is not practical to hike over Cape Johnson or Yellow Banks and they should be rounded at water level only on an outgoing or low tide. The three other headlands can be climbed over by scrambling across their low saddles along the route of World War II abandoned Coast Guard trails.

13. Indian Village Trail

About half of the distance is sandy beach. Of the remaining half, approximately one quarter of the distance is gravelly and one quarter over boulders. Many boulders are algae covered and exceedingly slick when wet. Boulder hopping is risky. It is safer to step carefully between boulders.

The hiker on this trail encounters a wide variety of scenery, sound, and odor. Over sea and headlands, skies change ceaselessly, while each new breeze brings with it the fragrance of kelp and salt air. On the land side is the silent green forest, seaward is the inward-marching surf, and above, the sea gulls keep up their steady complaint. Scrawled on the wet sands of the beaches are the signs of nocturnal visits of the forest animals. The stone memorials are a reminder of the fierce winter gales and of the sailors whose ships were blown onto the jagged reefs.

Map 9

La Push-Lower Hoh River

La Push Road

0.0 mi. U.S. 101, 2 mi. north of Forks and 53 mi. west of Port Angeles.

3.0   Junction with Quileute Road.

8.0   Junction with road to Rialto Beach.

12.0   Junction with road to Third Ocean Beach Trail and approach to the La Push-Hoh River Ocean Beach Way Trail.

13.6   Second Ocean Beach Trail.

14.0   First Ocean Beach Trail.

14.1   La Push Ocean Park.

14.2   Village of La Push.

The road goes mostly through logged-off lands to the Quileute Indian village of La Push, at the mouth of the Quileute River. Very little, if any, of the original Indian way of life remains. However, some Indians still use the cedar dugout canoes for setting their salmon nets.

Three short trails start from this road and lead to ocean beaches south of the village.

Rialto Beach Road

0.0 mi. La Push Road, 8 mi. from U.S. 101.
2.0   Junction with Quileute Road.
2.0   National Park boundary.
2.5   Mora Campground and Ranger Station. Information and backcountry use permits.
4.9   Rialto Ocean Beach picnic area.

This road branches off from the main road to La Push and crosses the Dickey River to the long sandy Rialto Beach.

Third Ocean Beach Trail

0.0 mi. Leaves La Push Road 12 mi. from U.S. 101.
0.9   The beach.
        Approximate hiking time: 20 to 30 minutes.

This is one of the finest sandy ocean beaches in the park; it is almost a mile in length.

From the south end of Third Beach the Ocean Beach Way Trail leads to the Hoh River (14.5 mi.).

Second Ocean Beach Trail

0.0 mi. La Push Road, 13.6 mi. from U.S. 101.
0.6   The beach.
        Approximate hiking time: 15 to 20 minutes.

This trail leads to an excellent sandy beach hemmed in on the south by Teahwhit Point and on the north by the headland immediately south of La Push. During winter storms this beach becomes strewn with glass balls which have drifted here from the coast of Japan.

First Ocean Beach Trail

0.0 mi. La Push Road, 14 mi. from U.S. 101.

0.2   The beach.

           Approximate hiking time: 5 minutes.

This short trail leads to the large sandy La Push Ocean Beach.

La Push-Hoh River Ocean Beach Way Trail

0.0 mi. End of Third Ocean Beach Trail, 0.9 mi. from La Push
           Road.

0.9   Start of trail across Taylor's Point.

2.1   Beach south of Taylor's Point.

2.7   Point No. 1.

2.9   Mouth of Scott Creek.

3.0   Point No. 2. Pass on outgoing tide.

4.3   Strawberry Point. Easily rounded.

5.5   Toleak Point. Easily rounded.

5.7   Mouth of Jackson Creek.

6.5   Junction with Goodman Creek Trail.

7.3   Goodman Creek. Hunt upstream for a crossing.

7.8   Beach.

10.1   Mouth of Mosquito Creek.

10.5   Point No. 3. Must be climbed over.

10.9   Point No. 4. Must be climbed over.

11.1   Point No. 5. Rounded only on low tide.

11.5   Point No. 6. Passable on low tide only, but can be
           climbed over. Start of trail across Hoh Head.

11.7   Point No. 7. Passable on low tide only, but can be
           climbed over.

12.2   Hoh Head.

12.6   End of the trail across Hoh Head.

13.3   Point No. 8. Rounded only on low tide.

14.5   Mouth of Hoh River.

    To reach the starting point of this trail take the Third Ocean
Beach Trail from La Push Road to the ocean.

    The trail across Taylor's Point is perhaps the most difficult
of the entire trip. Keep a sharp lookout for orange trail markers
especially where windfalls and brush have covered the trail. Even
though this way trail is brushed out periodically, the annual

MAP 9 57

growth of bracken fern and other plants can quickly obscure the trail. This trail, unlike most, runs along fallen logs in many places instead of keeping to ground level. During wet weather caution is essential since the logs are slippery. However, many of the logs have been notched and flattened on top for easier walking.

Half a mile south of Taylor's Point is Point No. 1. Climb up east over the top, then down the west side of the first valley parallel with the ocean, to the mouth of Scott Creek. A short distance beyond Scott Creek is Point No. 2, which can be rounded on an outgoing tide.

From Point No. 2 to the Goodman Creek Trail it is approximately 3.5 miles. Strawberry and Toleak points look quite formidable on the map, but they can be easily rounded.

Follow the Goodman Creek Trail inland to the crossing of Falls Creek. To cross Goodman Creek, find a log jam or cross during periods of low tide. From the south bank follow the orange markers back to the beach. Goodman Creek flows into the ocean between rock cliffs; this makes it necessary to cross the creek inland. From the mouth of Goodman Creek south to Mosquito Creek, again follow the beach. Mosquito Creek can be waded at low tide, when it is about a foot deep.

From Mosquito Creek follow the beach to Point No. 3 on the map. This point must be climbed over, to a bay and to Point No. 4, which also must be climbed over. A fair-sized creek runs into the small bay south of Point No. 4, and it must be waded. Point No. 5 should be rounded at low tide, as it is very difficult to climb over. From Point No. 5 a good sandy beach stretches south to 2 small points, Nos. 6 and 7, which are passable only at low tide. However, it is not impossible to climb over them. During high tides a marked way trail is available from Mosquito Creek to Hoh Head.

From Point 7 a long sandy beach stretches south to Hoh Head. At Point No. 6 leave the beach and climb east to the trail around the head.

From Hoh Head south to Point No. 8 is fair walking on the beach. Point No. 8 consists of a jumble of huge rocks which can only be rounded at low tide. From these rocks a narrow strip of beach, strewn with driftwood and boulders, extends over a

14. Third Beach

MAP 10   **59**

mile south to the Hoh River. From the mouth of the Hoh River way trails lead to the end of the Oil City Road, which takes you back to U.S. 101.

The trip should only be attempted by experienced hikers in the best physical condition.

Map 10

Kalaloch-Ruby Beach

U.S. 101

0.0 mi.	National Park boundary, 2 mi. north of Queets.
1.2	Ocean Beach Trail No. 1. 0.1 mi. to beach.
2.1	Ocean Beach Trail No. 2. 0.05 mi. to beach.
3.0	Kalaloch Ranger Station. Information and backcountry use permits.
3.1	Kalaloch Ocean Beach Village. Lodge, restaurant, housekeeping cabins, grocery store, and gasoline station.
3.3	Kalaloch Creek Trail. About 0.9 mi. to the park boundary.
3.5	Kalaloch Campground. Water, stoves, tables, and comfort stations.
5.3	Highway viewpoint. Automobile parking.
6.9	Ocean Beach Trail No. 3. 0.1 mi. to beach.
7.6	Ocean Beach Trail No. 4. 0.15 mi. to beach.
9.3	0.3 mi. to world's largest known western redcedar.
9.9	Ocean Beach Trail No. 6. 0.1 mi. to beach.
10.4	Ocean Beach Trail No. 7. 0.1 mi. to beach.
12.1	Ruby Beach.
14.2	National Park boundary.
15.0	Junction with Lower Hoh Road.

This section of the main highway follows the coast of the Pacific Coast Area. Seven short beach trails lead from the highway to the ocean. Each trail is distinct and different from the others. The vegetation growing near the salt air is of particular interest. The beaches themselves present changing scenes of great beauty. Uprooted trees lie like giants flung against shore and cliff. Isolated rock pillars tower above the waves, and the roar of the pounding, grinding surf indicates its immense power.

Surfcasting and, in season, clamming, crabbing, and smelt fishing are very popular along this stretch of the coast. Check with the park ranger for seasons and limits.

Map 11

Bogachiel River

North Shore Bogachiel River Road

This road leaves U.S. 101 near Bogachiel State Park, about 5.5 miles south of Forks. It follows the north side of the Bogachiel River about 3 miles. From here a trail leads 2 miles to the boundary of Olympic National Park. This road leads through logged-off lands to the Bogachiel River rain forest. The road frequently washes out, and it is often impossible to drive to the end.

Upper Hoh River Road

0.0 mi.   U.S. 101, 14 mi. south of Forks.
9.3   Village of Spruce. Grocery store, gasoline, and cabins.
12.8   National Park boundary.
13.0   Bogachiel-Hoh Trail to Bogachiel River Trail (11 mi. or 11.6 mi.).

MAP 11 61

18.9   Hoh Rain Forest Campground.
19.0   Hoh Visitor Center and end of Hoh River Road. Information, exhibits, and backcountry use permits.

Outside the park boundary the road passes through logged-off land. From the boundary to the end of the road it runs through a fine example of rain forest, with groves of large Sitka spruce and western hemlock intermingled with moss-covered bigleaf and vine maple and scatterings of Douglas-fir and western red-cedar.

The Hoh valley is a late fall and winter foraging area for the Roosevelt elk, which usually summer in the high country of the interior. It is a favorite area for viewing the elk herds, as even in the summer some will occasionally be seen feeding in the valley.

South Fork Hoh River Road

0.0 mi. Allen Logging Co. at U.S. 101.
16.0   End of the road and start of South Fork Hoh River Trail.

This road begins as a wide, graded logging mainline (Road #H-1000) from the south side of U.S. 101 at Allen Logging Co. The road gradually narrows near the end after crossing the South Fork of the Hoh River, and the trailhead is a short distance beyond.

Bogachiel River Trail

0.0 mi. National Park boundary, 5 mi. from U.S. 101.
4.1   Junction with Indian Pass Trail to Sitkum River Forest Service Road (8.4 mi.).
4.2   Bogachiel camp.
6.2   Bogachiel-Hoh Trail. From here it is 11.6 mi. to Upper Hoh River Road.
8.3   Flapjack camp.
12.4   Fifteen Mile camp.
15.4   Hyak camp.
18.6   Twenty-one Mile camp.

20.1   Slide Pass (3300) (Map 7).

22.8   Junction with Mink Lake Trail to Upper Soleduck River-Hot Springs Road (4.3 mi.) (Map 7).

26.4   Junction with Deer Lake-Bogachiel Peak Trail at Deer Lake (Map 7).

The Bogachiel River Trail follows an easy grade to the point where it starts to climb to Slide Pass. It is through typical rain forest with Sitka spruce and western hemlock dominating, although Douglas-firs and western redcedars are present.

From Slide Pass to the Deer Lake-Bogachiel Peak Trail the Bogachiel River Trail follows along the ridge through alternating open meadow and subalpine fir forest. Blackwood and Bogachiel lakes both contain eastern brook trout.

The Bogachiel Valley is a wild and primitive area offering numerous opportunities for seeing wildlife. Roosevelt elk range in the river bottoms during the winter and in the high country during the summer. Deer and bears can often be seen, while cougars, bobcats, and many smaller animals can sometimes be spotted by the experienced woodsman.

The Bogachiel River offers good fishing both summer and winter with its sea-run steelhead and cutthroat trout.

Indian Pass Trail

0.0 mi.   Bogachiel River Trail, 4.1 mi. from park boundary.

1.8   Indian Pass (1041).

3.4   South Fork Calawah River.

6.3   Rugged Ridge and Park boundary.

This up-and-down trail crosses 3 river valleys and 3 ridges. It climbs from the Bogachiel Valley about 600 feet to the top of Indian Pass. From Indian Pass it drops 300 feet to the South Fork Calawah River. Here the trail becomes a way trail to the top of Rugged Ridge, which is a 550-foot climb.

15. Forest colonnade, Hoh River valley

Bogachiel-Hoh Trail

0.0 mi. Bogachiel River Trail, 6.2 mi. from park boundary.
11.6   Upper Hoh River Road.
         Approximate hiking time: 5 to 6 hours.

The trail climbs to the top of a north-south ridge which it follows to the Hoh River valley. It is in the forest most of the way, although there is an excellent view of Mt. Olympus from the ridge. As you climb out of the Bogachiel River valley, the dominant Sitka spruce and western hemlock gradually change to Douglas-fir and western hemlock above 1000 feet.

Little drinking water is available on the ridge.

Map 12

Hoh River and South Fork Hoh River

South Fork Hoh River Trail

0.0 mi. South Fork Hoh River Road.
0.25   National Park boundary.
1.0   Big Flat.
4.5   End of maintained trail.
6.5   Last 2 mi. way trail.

At the park boundary the trail enters the forest and continues to Big Flat. From this point the route goes through typical rain forest containing Sitka spruce, western hemlock, black cottonwood, western red alder, and maple. The South Fork Hoh River is reported to be a good trout stream and has summer and winter runs of both steelhead and salmon.

Hoh River Trail

0.0 mi. Hoh Ranger Station at end of the Upper Hoh River Road.

MAP 12 **65**

2.7   Junction with Tom Creek Way Trail (1.2 mi.).

5.4   Happy Four.

8.7   Olympus Guard Station.

9.5   Junction with Hoh Lake Trail to Deer Lake-Bogachiel Peak Trail (6.5 mi.).

14.2   Elk Lake.

16.6   Glacier Meadows.

17.1   Terminus of Blue Glacier, end of trail.

This trail leads through some of the finest examples of rain forest in the park. Sitka spruce and western hemlock are the dominant forest trees, while Douglas-fir and western redcedar are subdominant. Under the Sitka spruce, some of which tower 300 feet, are the understories of bigleaf maple, vine maple, shrubs, ferns, and mosses.

The rain forest is not dark and gloomy, as one might think. Sun shining on the heavy covering of mosses on the ground and the tree trunks fills the woods with a soft green light, and the forest can change its mood with each change of weather. Because of browsing by the elk, the forest floor is fairly free of thick underbrush.

The hiker may see Roosevelt elk grazing in the river bottoms. Small animals also inhabit the rain forest, but they are less often seen. Birds singing high in the treetops can often be heard from the trail.

The Hoh River Trail provides the easiest way to Mt. Olympus. It follows river grade to Glacier Creek, then starts a steeper climb from here to Glacier Meadows, where the ascent of Mt. Olympus begins. Only experienced, properly equipped climbers in excellent physical condition should climb Mt. Olympus (7965). Although Glacier Meadows can be reached in one day, a more enjoyable trip is assured if 2 days are allowed to cover the 16.6 miles.

Hall of Mosses and Spruce Nature Trails

0.0 mi. The Visitor Center at the end of the Upper Hoh River Road.

0.85 and 1.3, respectively.

Approximate walking time: 45 minutes and 1 hour, respectively, to as much time as you have available.

These loop trails will help you to understand the Olympic Rain Forest. Self-guiding signs along the way interpret the rain forest communities.

Tom Creek Way Trail

0.0 mi. Hoh River Trail, 2.7 mi. up.

1.2   End of the trail.

Approximate hiking time: 1.5 to 2 hours.

This trail fords the Hoh River just beyond the mouth of Tom Creek and follows the east side of the creek.

Hoh Lake Trail

0.0 mi. Hoh River Trail, 0.6 mi. above Olympus Guard Station.

5.3   Hoh Lake (4600).

6.5   Deer Lake-Bogachiel Peak Trail. From this junction it is 8.3 mi. to the Upper Soleduck River-Hot Springs Road (Map 7).

Approximate hiking time: 4 to 5 hours.

It is a steep climb to High Divide and the end of the Deer Lake-Bogachiel Peak Trail.

Map 13

Queets River

Queets River Road

0.0 mi. U.S. 101, 20 mi. north of Quinault and 7 mi. south of Queets.

16. Queets River, with Mt. Olympus in background

0.5   National Park boundary.

12.5   Queets River Ranger Station. Information and back-
         country use permits, summer.

13.5   Queets River Campground. Stoves, tables, and sanitary
         facilities. Start of Campground Loop Trail.

14.0   End of Queets River Road.

This road goes through a narrow river-bottom corridor which
has been partially logged off. On clear days there are many fine
vistas to the distant mountains.

The Queets River is famous for its excellent fishing in season,
especially summer and winter steelheading and late summer sea-
run cutthroat and salmon fishing.

Queets River Campground Loop Trail

0.0 mi. Queets River Campground.

3.0   Round trip.

         Approximate hiking time: 1 to 1.5 hours.

Starting from the campground, the trail follows the Queets
River west and then cuts south across the Queets River Road. It
passes through several open field areas and finally returns to the
campground on the Sams River Trail. Small herds of elk are
often seen in open fields along the trail.

Sams River Trail

0.0 mi. Near the end of the Queets River Road.

0.9   The end of the maintained trail.

         Approximate hiking time: 0.75 to 1 hour.

The first part of the trail runs near the river and is subject to
frequent washouts. It is a good route for fishermen.

Queets River Trail

0.0 mi. End of Queets River Road and river ford.

2.3   Junction with Kloochman Rock Way Trail.

3.9   Junction with lower Tshletshy Creek Way Trail crossing
         on Queets River.

5.0   Spruce Bottom.

MAP 13   **69**

5.6   Junction with upper Tshletshy Creek Way Trail crossing on Queets River.

11.1   Bob Creek.

15.5   Pelton Creek. End of the trail.

The trail up the Queets Valley can only be reached by wading across the river near the end of the road. The river is fairly wide and swift at this point. Wading involves crossing in water above the knees in depth and on a slippery, rocky stream bottom. While a safe crossing can be made during low water periods in late summer and fall, there are times when the river is too deep and swift to wade, particularly in spring and early summer or after heavy winter rains.

The trail follows the river at a very easy, even grade for the full length of the trail. The valley floor contains giant Sitka spruce, moss draped maples and open, parklike areas in which herds of elk are often seen. Summer and winter steelhead fishing is good at times. Salmon, sea-run cutthroat, and rainbow trout are also caught during the summer and fall.

Kloochman Rock Way Trail

0.0 mi. Queets River Trail, 2.3 mi. up.

3.4   End of the trail.

Approximate hiking time: 1.5 to 2 hours.

This trail leads up from the valley floor to a high vantage point with excellent views of Hoh Peak and Mt. Tom to the east and Colonel Bob to the south. The largest known Douglas-fir tree is to be found about 0.1 mile west of this trail and 0.2 mile from the Queets River. The diameter of this tree is 14 feet, 6 inches, at chest height, and its height is 221 feet.

Tshletshy Creek Way Trail

0.0 mi. Upper junction with Queets River Trail.

16.0   Tshletshy-Big Creek Divide. From this point it is 0.2 mi. to Three Lakes, 0.5 mi. to Skyline Trail, and 7.1 mi. to North Shore and North Fork Quinault River Road (Maps 14, 15).

This is a rough, up and down trail for most of the 16 miles. For the most part the trail leads through western hemlock and grand fir with a few scattered Douglas-fir. Two miles before the divide the trail breaks out into open meadow and subalpine fir country. Late summer runs of steelhead and salmon make this stream a favorite with anglers.

Map 14

Lake Quinault

North Fork Quinault River Road

0.0 mi. U.S. 101, 46 mi. north of Hoquiam.

3.9   July Creek Campground. Water, stoves, tables, and sanitary facilities.

5.8   Ranger station. Information, backcountry use permits.

14.2   Junction with South Shore and Quinault River Road. Bunch Creek bridge across main Quinault River.

17.1   Three Lakes Trail. From here it is 6.6 mi. to junction with Skyline Trail.

18.2   North Fork Campground (undeveloped).

18.6   North Fork Ranger Station. Information and backcountry use permits in summer.

This road through the woods above the shores of Lake Quinault offers glimpses now and then of the lake. The lake itself is in the Quinault Indian Reservation. The road passes several farms and logged-off areas up to the Bunch Creek bridge which crosses the main Quinault River to the South Shore and Quinault Road. The route from the bridge to the end of the road is through Sitka spruce and western hemlock forest.

Quinault River Road

0.0 mi. U.S. 101, 43 mi. north of Hoquiam.

1.5   Willaby Creek Forest Service campground. Water, stoves, tables, and sanitary facilities.

17. Red Alder

2.0   Town of Quinault.
2.4   Falls Creek Forest Service campground. Water, stoves, tables, and sanitary facilities.
7.0   Colonel Bob Trail to summit of Colonel Bob (6.5 mi.).
11.9   National Park boundary.
12.9   Bunch Creek bridge across Quinault River to North Fork Quinault River Road.
18.6   Graves Creek Ranger Station; backcountry use permits, summer (Map 15).
18.8   Graves Creek Campground (Map 15). Community kitchen, water, stoves, tables, and sanitary facilities.
19.3   Graves Creek Trail to Six Ridge Pass (8.9 mi.) (Maps 1, 15, 16).
21.6   End of the road and start of Quinault River-Enchanted Valley Trail (Maps 15, 16).

This road goes through the town of Quinault and the U.S. Forest Service Lake Quinault Recreational Area, where there are several interesting trails, as well as boating, swimming, and fishing in Lake Quinault. There are 2 U.S. Forest Service campgrounds and a Forest Service ranger station on the south shore of Lake Quinault; also in this area are several cabin resorts and picturesque Lake Quinault Lodge, with modern coffee shop and dining room.

Leaving the lake, the road winds up the Quinault valley past several small farms to a dense stand of rain forest. About 13 miles from U.S. 101 a bridge crosses the main Quinault River to the road up the north fork of the Quinault River to the ranger station. From the point where the main river branches into the east and north forks, the east fork road goes through some of the finest examples of rain forest in the park.

Three Lakes Trail

0.0 mi. North Fork Quinault River Road, 2.9 mi. above Bunch Creek Bridge.
6.6   Junction with Skyline Trail.
7.1   Tshletshy-Big Creek divide.
         Approximate hiking time: 3.5 to 4 hours.

MAP 15 **73**

This trail goes past Irely Lake (1.1 mile), a good early-season lowland fishing lake. It then starts to climb a forested ridge to the Big Creek-Tshletshy divide where it meets the Tshletshy Creek Way Trail (7.1 miles) leading to the Queets River (16.3 miles) (Map 13). The last few miles of this trail are in subalpine fir forest and meadow country. It is often possible to see elk in the vicinity of the Three Lakes. There are no trout in these ponds.

Map 15

North Fork Quinault River-Low Divide

Quinault River Road

See discussion under Map 14.

North Fork Quinault River-Low Divide Trail

0.0 mi. North Fork Quinault River Road, at end.
2.5   Wolf Bar.
6.5   Junction with Elip Creek Trail to Skyline Trail (4.6 mi.).
7.0   Francis Creek camp.
8.5   Trapper camp.
11.5   Twelve Mile camp.
12.3   Sixteen Mile.
15.9   Junction with Skyline Trail. From this junction it is 20.3 mi. to Three Lakes Trail and 26.9 mi. to the North Shore and North Fork Quinault River Road, on Skyline and Three Lakes trails.
16.1   Low Divide Guard Station.
16.4   Low Divide (3600). Junction with Low Divide Trail to Elwha River Trail (2.6 mi.) (Map 6). It is 28.4 mi. from Low Divide to Whiskey Bend (Maps 5, 6).

This trail follows the west side of the North Fork Quinault River through an excellent example of rain forest. Sitka spruce and western hemlock predominate except in the river bottoms with their groves of moss-covered bigleaf maples, red alders, and black cottonwoods. The trail follows the river grade, except for 5 or 6 ridge points which it climbs. Through several sections of narrow canyons the trail is 200 to 300 feet above the river. Midway along the trail is a large blow-down area with uprooted trees lying in every direction. The trail crosses the river at Sixteen Mile and starts a 4.1 mile climb to Low Divide (3600), where there are several large open meadows. During the summer months it is often possible to see elk, bear, deer, and marmots in these meadows. The usual display of subalpine flowers follows the melting snows.

From Low Divide side trips can be made to Martins Park (1.0), Martins Lakes (2.3), and Mt. Seattle (3.5). See discussion under Map 6.

Elip Creek Trail

0.0 mi. North Fork Quinault River Trail, 6.5 mi. up.
4.6   Skyline Trail.
          Approximate hiking time: 2 to 3 hours.

This trail makes possible a 20.6-mile loop trip from the end of the North Shore and North Fork Quinault River Road, on the North Fork Quinault River, Elip Creek, Skyline, and Three Lakes trails. The route goes through both rain forest and high country in less distance than is possible elsewhere in this area. Elk can often be seen in the alpine meadows along the Skyline Trail.

Skyline Trail *(rough way trail from Low Divide to Kimta Peak)*

0.0 mi. North Fork Quinault River Trail, 15.9 mi. up.
4.0   Seattle Creek.
6.5   Lake Beauty.
9.5   Promise Creek Divide.
11.0   Kimta Peak.
16.0   Three Prune.
17.5   Junction with Elip Creek Trail.
20.3   Terminus at junction with Three Lakes Trail. From here it is 6.6 mi. to North Fork Quinault River Road.

This trail is continuously in high country from Low Divide to the Three Lakes Trail. From Low Divide the trail climbs for

MAP 15 75

about 1.5 miles through mature subalpine fir forest to near the top of the ridge running south from Mt. Seattle. From here to the Seattle Creek Basin the trail meanders through extensive heather meadows on the east side of Mt. Seattle. By a series of switchbacks the trail drops down 400 feet through subalpine fir forest to the upper part of the basin near towering Mt. Noyes. Swinging around the west side of the basin it climbs now as a way trail on an easy grade through subalpine fir forest and open heather meadows to a 4700-foot saddle on the Quinault-Queets Divide. Crossing this saddle the way enters the Queets River drainage and contours through alternate subalpine fir forest and meadow country to Lake Beauty, then continues on the west slope for approximately 1 mile beyond Lake Beauty. From here it climbs 400 feet to the top of a higher part of the divide and contours along the east side to the head of Promise Creek. The section from Lake Beauty to the head of Promise Creek is poorly marked but goes through more or less open meadow country, and it should not be too difficult to find the way. When traveling from the direction of the Three Lakes Trail, be careful not to follow a well-beaten trail leading down into the Promise Creek Basin. This trail goes but a short distance and then ends, and a rough, partially blazed way trail continues down to a junction with the North Fork Quinault River Trail 4.0 miles below Low Divide.

From the head of Promise Creek to Kimta Peak the Skyline Trail follows more or less the 5000-foot contour on the east side of the divide. From Kimta Peak to the Three Lakes Trail the route is through alternating meadow and subalpine fir forest. This section contains many fine views of the beautiful basins of Stalding Creek, Three Prune Creek, and others. In late summer and early fall herds of Roosevelt elk can be seen along this trail. Black bears are also quite numerous, especially in huckleberry season.

The Skyline Trail follows a main ridge which is the divide between the Quinault and Queets watersheds. The views across these watersheds to the mountain ranges beyond are excellent. Because of heavy winter snowfall in this area, this trip is not recommended until August and September.

18. Along the Hoh River

Map 16

Quinault River-Enchanted Valley

Graves Creek Trail

0.0 mi. Quinault River Road, 19.3 mi. from U.S. 101.
6.1   Junction with trail to Wynoochee Pass (1.5 mi.).
7.5   Junction with trail to Sundown Pass (0.5 mi.).
7.8   Lake Sundown.
8.9   Six Ridge Pass (4600). From here it is 11.7 mi. to North Fork Skokomish River Road (Map 1).

This trail climbs up and follows above the north side of the Graves Creek canyon to its confluence with Success Creek. It then crosses to the west side and goes through the forest some distance above the creek, which it again crosses after reaching Graves Creek Basin. This basin is a favorite summer elk grazing area. Lake Sundown lies in the upper basin in a beautiful alpine meadow.

Quinault River-Enchanted Valley Trail

0.0 mi. End of Quinault River Road, 19.3 mi. from U.S. 101.
7.5   O'Neil Creek camp.
13.5   Enchanted Valley Ranger Station.
15.4   Largest known western hemlock. The circumference of this tree is 27 feet, 2 inches, at chest height.
16.7   O'Neil Pass Trail to O'Neil Pass (7.4 mi.) and the Duckabush River Road (28.4 mi.) (Map 2).
18.3   Anderson Pass (4464). Junction with trail to Anderson Glacier. From the pass it is 10.6 mi. to the Dosewallips River Road (Map 2).

This trail goes through typical valley rain forest consisting of scattered groups of Sitka spruce and western hemlock and groves of moss-covered maples, red alders, and black cottonwoods. The trail grade is gradual except where it crosses a few ridge points.

Enchanted Valley, sometimes called the "Valley of Ten Thousand Waterfalls," is true "storybook" country. Its many beauties are difficult to describe, and it gives one a feeling of a scene from a child's fairytale. One mile beyond the ranger station the trail starts a climb to Anderson Pass. On the way to the pass are close-up views of the hanging glacier at the head of Anderson Creek. Elk are commonly seen between Enchanted Valley and Anderson Pass. Goats can usually be seen, with the help of field glasses, on the precipitous walls of Enchanted Valley.

O'Neil Pass Trail

0.0 mi.   Quinault River-Enchanted Valley, 16.7 mi. up.
7.4   O'Neil Pass *(not suitable for stock)*. From the pass it is
          21.0 mi. to the Duckabush River Road.
          Approximate hiking time: 3.5 to 4 hours.

The first 2.5 miles are a steady climb through alternating high-country subalpine fir forest and meadow. The trail then levels off and contours along the side of the ridge which is the divide between the Duckabush and Quinault River valleys. As the trail climbs, magnificent views of Mt. Anderson and its glaciers come into view. The floral display in the large subalpine meadows is quite late in the season, usually during the months of August and September. During this short period a floral procession of color follows the snow melt. Large herds of Roosevelt elk make their summer home in these high-country meadows.

19. Olympic elk in the Queets River valley

INDEX

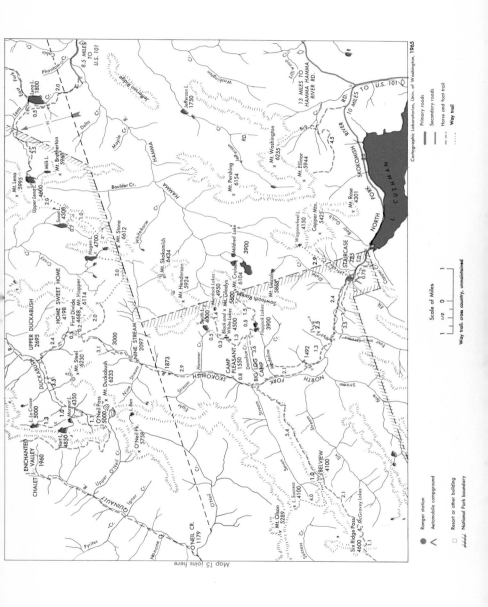

Cartographic Laboratories, Univ. of Washington, 1965

Primary roads
Secondary roads
Horse and foot trail
Way trail

● Ranger station
∧ Automobile campground
□ Resort or other building
▨ National Park boundary

Scale of Miles

Way trail, cross country, unmaintained

Map 15 joins here

8.5 MILES TO U.S. 101
13 MILES TO HAMMA HAMMA RIVER RD.
10 MILES TO U.S. 101

L. CUSHMAN
NORTH FORK SKOKOMISH RIVER RD.

ENCHANTED VALLEY
CHALET 1960

UPPER DUCKABUSH 2695
HOME SWEET HOME 4198

First Divide

Mt. Hopper 6114
Mt. Steel 6230
Mt. Duckabush 6233

L. La Crosse 5000
Hart L. 4850
Marmot L. 4350
O'Neil Pass 5000
O'Neil Pk. 5758
L. Ben

O'NEIL CR. 1179
Pyrites
Nonname Cr.
Upper O'Neil Cr.
Ignar Cr.

Mt. Olson 5289
BELVIEW 4100
Six Ridge Pass 4600
McGravey Lakes

Success Cr.
Seven Stream
Six Stream
Five Stream
Four Stream
Three Stream

NORTH FORK

BIG LOG CAMP
CAMP PLEASANT
Donahue Cr.
Madeline Cr.

Flapjack Lakes 3900
Sawtooth Ridge 5868
Mt. Lincoln 5868
Mt. Cruiser 6104
Ruby
Black and White Lakes 4950
Mt. Gladys 5600
Smith L.
Murdock Lakes
Mt. Henderson 5924
Mt. Skokomish 6434

Mildred Lake 3900

NINE STREAM 2097
Nine Stream
Eight Stream
Hammer Cr.

SKOKOMISH

Mt. Stone 6612
Scout L. 4300
Higgen L. 4700
Whitehorse Cr.

Wagonwheel L.
L. Success 5425
Copper Mtn. 5425
Copper Gulch

STAIRCASE 785
Slate Cr.
Elk Cr.
Four Stream

Mt. Rose 4301
Mt. Ellinor 5944
Mt. Washington 6255
Mt. Pershing 6154

HAMMA
HAMMA
Boulder Cr.
Maple Cr.
Washington Cr.

Jefferson L. 1750

Mt. Bretherton 5960
Mt. Lena 5995
Milk L.
Upper Lena L. 4600

Lena L. 1800
Lena East Fork
Phantom Cr.

Jefferson Ridge
Delta Cr.

MAP 2

DOSEWALLIPS—DUCKABUSH RIVER

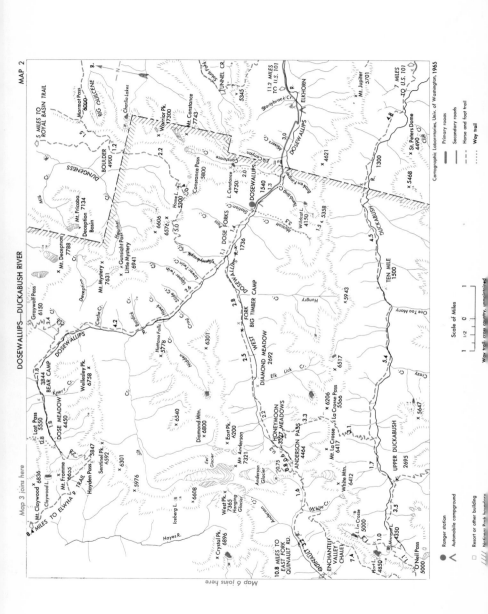

Cartographic Laboratories, Univ. of Washington, 1965

Primary roads

Secondary roads

Horse and foot trail

Way trail

Ranger station

Automobile campground

Resort or other building

National Park boundary

Way trail; cross country, unmaintained

Scale of Miles

1   1/2   0   1

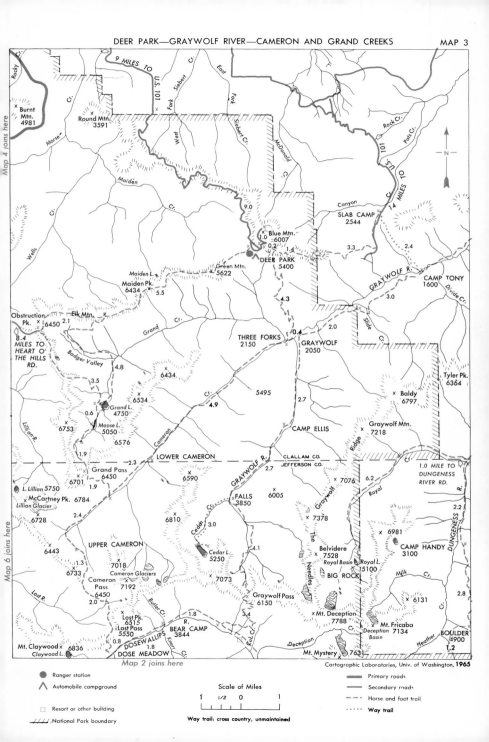

Map 4 joins here

Map 6 joins here

9 MILES TO U.S. 101

14 MILES TO U.S. 101

x Burnt Mtn. 4981

Round Mtn. 3591

Rocky Cr.

Morse Cr.

Siebert Fork

West Fork

East Fork

Siebert Cr.

McDonald Cr.

Rock Cr.

Post Cr.

Maiden Cr.

Wells Cr.

9.0

Canyon

SLAB CAMP 2544

3.3

2.4

x Blue Mtn. 6007

1.0

0.2

1.4

DEER PARK 5400

GRAYWOLF R.

CAMP TONY 1600

Divide Cr.

Maiden L.

Maiden Pk. 6434

x Green Mtn. 5622

5.5

4.3

3.0

Obstruction Pk. x 6450

Elk Mtn. 2.1

8.4 MILES TO HEART O' THE HILLS RD.

Grand Cr.

THREE FORKS 2150

0.4

2.0

GRAYWOLF 2050

Slide Cr.

Tyler Pk. 6364

Badger Valley

4.8

x 6434

5495

2.7

x Baldy 6797

3.5

x 6534

4.9

CAMP ELLIS

x Graywolf Mtn. 7218

Grand L. 4750

0.6

Moose L. 5050

6576

Cameron Cr.

Lillian R.

x 6753

1.9

2.3

LOWER CAMERON

GRAYWOLF R.

CLALLAM CO.
JEFFERSON CO.

2.7

Ridge

Cr.

1.0 MILE TO DUNGENESS RIVER RD.

Grand Pass 6450

x 6590

x 7076

6.2

Royal Cr.

DUNGENESS R.

L. Lillian 5750

x 6701

1.9

FALLS 3850

x 6005

Graywolf

2.2

McCartney Pk. 6784

Lillian Glacier

2.4

x 6728

x 6810

Cedar Cr.

3.0

4.1

x 7378

x 6981

CAMP HANDY 3100

2.8

UPPER CAMERON

1.3

x 6443

Cedar L. 5250

The Needles

Belvidere x 7528

Royal Basin

Royal L. 5100

BIG ROCK

Milk Cr.

x 6131

7018

Cameron Glaciers

x 7073

Cameron Pass 6450

6733

2.0

Butler Cr.

1.8

Graywolf Pass 6150

x Mt. Deception 7788

x Mt. Fricaba 7134

Deception Basin

BOULDER 4900

Heather Cr.

1.2

Lost R.

Lost Pk. 6615

Lost Pass 5550

BEAR CAMP 3844

3.4

Bull Cr.

Deception Cr.

Mt. Claywood x 6836

0.8

1.8

DOSEWALLIPS R.

Claywood L.

DOSE MEADOW

Mt. Mystery x 7631

● Ranger station

▲ Automobile campground

☐ Resort or other building

//// National Park boundary

Scale of Miles

1   1/2   0   1

Way trail: cross country, unmaintained

———— Primary roads

———— Secondary roads

- - - - Horse and foot trail

· · · · Way trail

N

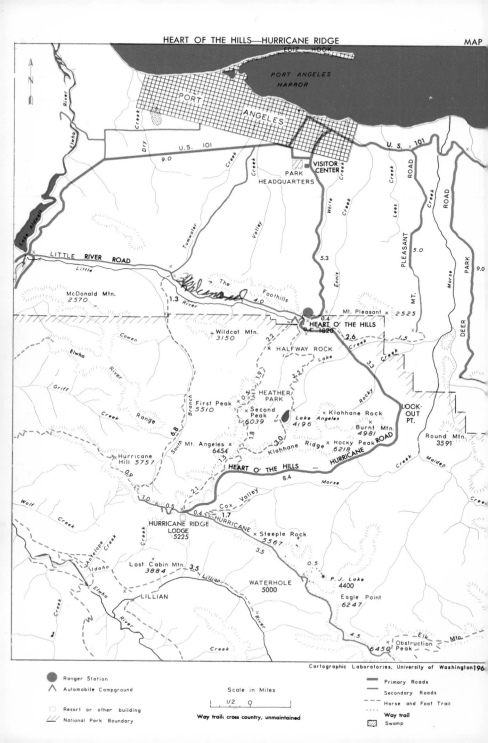

EDIZ HOOK

PORT ANGELES HARBOR

PORT ANGELES

U.S. 101
9.0

U.S. 101

PLEASANT MT. ROAD

PARK HEADQUARTERS

VISITOR CENTER

Dry Creek

Tumwater Creek

Valley Creek

White Creek

Ennis Creek

Lees Creek

Morse Creek

DEER PARK ROAD
5.0
9.0

LITTLE RIVER ROAD

Little River

McDonald Mtn. 2570

The Foothills

1.3   4.0

5.3

Mt. Pleasant × 2525

HEART O' THE HILLS
0.4 1820
0.4   2.6   1.3

Cowen

Elwha River

Griff Creek

Range

South Branch

6.8

Lake Aldwell

Elwha River

× Wildcat Mtn. 3150

2.2

HALFWAY ROCK

1.9

HEATHER PARK

× First Peak 5510

× Second Peak 6039

1.8

× Mt. Angeles 6454

1.5

× Hurricane Hill 5757

0.9

3.2

Lake

3.3

Rocky Creek

LOOK-OUT PT.

Lake Angeles 4196

× Klahhane Rock

× Burnt Mtn. 4981

Klahhane Ridge

× Rocky Peak 6218

Round Mtn. 3591

3.0

HEART O' THE HILLS — HURRICANE ROAD
8.4

Morse

Maiden Creek

1.0   0.5   2.1

Cox   Valley
0.4   1.7

HURRICANE

HURRICANE RIDGE LODGE 5225

× Steeple Rock 5567

3.5

Lost Cabin Mtn. 3884   3.5

Lillian River

WATERHOLE 5000

0.5

P.J. Lake 4400

Eagle Point 6247

Wolf Creek

Antelope Creek

Idaho Creek

Elwha River

LILLIAN

Creek

4.5

× 6450 Obstruction Peak

Elk Mtn.

● Ranger Station

⋀ Automobile Campground

▢ Resort or other building

▨ National Park Boundary

Scale in Miles

1/2   0

Way trail: cross country, unmaintained

━━━ Primary Roads

- - - Secondary Roads

· · · Horse and Foot Trail

Way trail

▨ Swamp

Hughes Cr.

2.5
Boulder L.
Boulder Pk. 5800
X 4450
Three Horse Lakes
2.8
Everett Pk. 5300
Blue L.
Mud L.
X Mt. Appleton 6140
HAPPY
Crystal
Happy L. 4850
2.5
0.5
HAPPY LAKE RIDGE
Hell Cr.
Cougar Cr.
Deep Cr.
0.6

ELWHA R.
2.0
McDonald Mtn.
1.0
2.6
2.0
ELWHA

2.6
Appleton Pass 5000
4.6
UPPER SOLEDUCK
Oyster L.
SOLEDUCK R.

BOULDER CREEK
Boulder Cr.
3.1
Deep Cr.
Cr.
4.5
OLYMPIC HOT SPRINGS RD.
2.5
1.2
ALTAIRE
0.1
1.0
ELWHA
2.8

2.5
0.8
OBSERVATION PT. 1387
1.0
WHISKEY BEND
MILLS
5.0
Sege Cr.
6.1
ELWHA RIVER RANGE

Cr.
0.4
Hurricane Cr.
WHISKEY BEND 1160
Fitzhenry Cr.
Wolf Cr.
1.5
HURRICANE HILL 5757
0.9
1.0

Cat Cr.
Haggerty Cr.
Mt. Fitzhenry 6105
0.3
2.0
Antelope Cr.
1.8
Idaho Cr.
2.3
Cr.
HURRICANE RIDGE LODGE
X 3884
5225
0.5

CL. ALLAM CO.
JEFFERSON CO.
Mt. Carrie X 7015
0.6
LILLIAN 1273
Lillian R.
3.5

Stephen Pk. 6430
Cream L.
Long Cr.
APPROXIMATE COUNTY BOUNDARY
9.9
4.1
Bowman Cr.
ELWHA R.
Windfall Cr.
Dorothy Cr.
Prescott Cr.

MARYS FALLS CAMP 1242
Mt. Ferry 6220
Ludden Pk. 5860 X
2.0
0.4
0.5
DODGER PT. 5759
1.7
Wildrose Cr.
CANYON CAMP
X 6534

1.0
1384
ELKHORN 1450
4.7
STONY POINT CAMP
0.2
McCartney Cr.
Mt. Scott X 5905
Stony Cr.
1.3

Goldie R.

Map 6 joins here

Cartographic Laboratories, Univ. of Washington, 1965

Scale of Miles
1   1/2   0   1

Way trail: cross country, unmaintained

● Ranger station
∧ Automobile campground
□ Resort or other building
//// National Park boundary

━━━ Primary roads
─── Secondary roads
- - - Horse and foot trail
····· Way trail

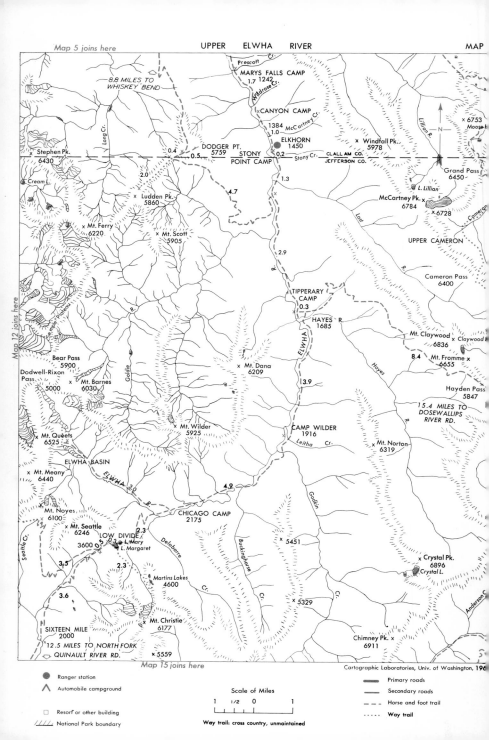

Map 5 joins here

8.8 MILES TO
WHISKEY BEND

Prescott Cr.

MARYS FALLS CAMP
1.7 1242

Wildrose Cr.

CANYON CAMP

McCartney Cr.

1384
1.0

ELKHORN
1450

× Windfall Pk.
5978

× 6753
Moose L

Long Cr.

× Stephen Pk.
6430

0.4

DODGER PT.
5759

STONY
POINT CAMP

0.5

0.2

Stony Cr.

CLALL AM CO.
JEFFERSON CO.

Lillian R.

N

Cream L.

2.0

1.3

Grand Pass
6450

× Ludden Pk.
5860

4.7

× L. Lillian

McCartney Pk. ×
6784

× 6728

Cameron R.

× Mt. Ferry
6220

× Mt. Scott
5905

2.9

UPPER CAMERON

Cameron Pass
6400

Map 12 joins here

TIPPERARY
CAMP
0.3

HAYES R.
1685

ELWHA

Mt. Claywood ×
6836

× Claywood

8.4

Mt. Fromme ×
6655

Bear Pass
5900

Dodwell-Rixon
Pass
5000

× Mt. Barnes
6030

Goldie R.

× Mt. Dana
6209

13.9

Hayes R.

Hayden Pass
5847

15.4 MILES TO
DOSEWALLIPS
RIVER RD.

× Mt. Queets
6525

× Mt. Wilder
5925

CAMP WILDER
1916

Leitha Cr.

× Mt. Norton
6319

ELWHA BASIN

× Mt. Meany
6440

ELWHA R.

3.0

4.9

Godkin R.

× Mt. Noyes
6100

CHICAGO CAMP
2175

Seattle Cr.

× Mt. Seattle
6246

3600

LOW DIVIDE
0.3

2.3

L. Mary

L. Margaret

Delabarre Cr.

Buckinghorse Cr.

× 5451

× Crystal Pk.
6896

Crystal L.

3.5

2.3

Martins Lakes
4600

× 5329

Anderson C

3.6

× Mt. Christie
6177

Chimney Pk. ×
6911

SIXTEEN MILE
2000

12.5 MILES TO NORTH FORK
QUINAULT RIVER RD.

× 5559

Map 15 joins here

Cartographic Laboratories, Univ. of Washington, 196

● Ranger station

⋀ Automobile campground

☐ Resort or other building

//// National Park boundary

Scale of Miles

1   1/2   0   1

Way trail: cross country, unmaintained

Primary roads

Secondary roads

Horse and foot trail

Way trail

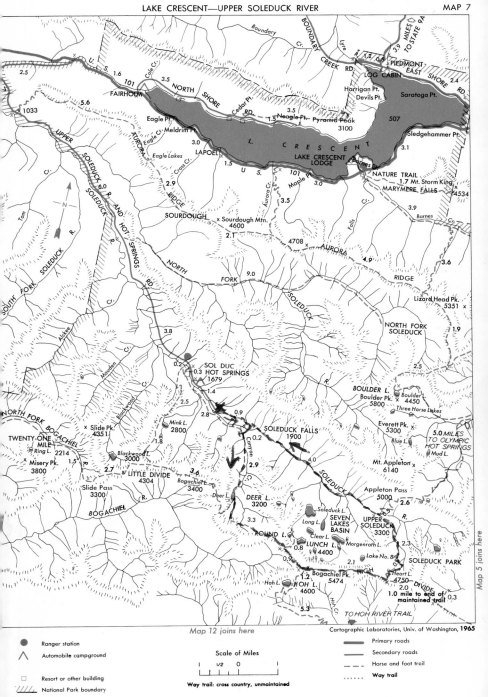

Map 12 joins here

Cartographic Laboratories, Univ. of Washington, 1965

Scale of Miles

```
    1    1/2    0                    1
```

Way trail: cross country, unmaintained

- ● Ranger station
- ∧ Automobile campground
- ☐ Resort or other building
- ////// National Park boundary

- ━━━ Primary roads
- ──── Secondary roads
- ─ ─ ─ Horse and foot trail
- ······ Way trail

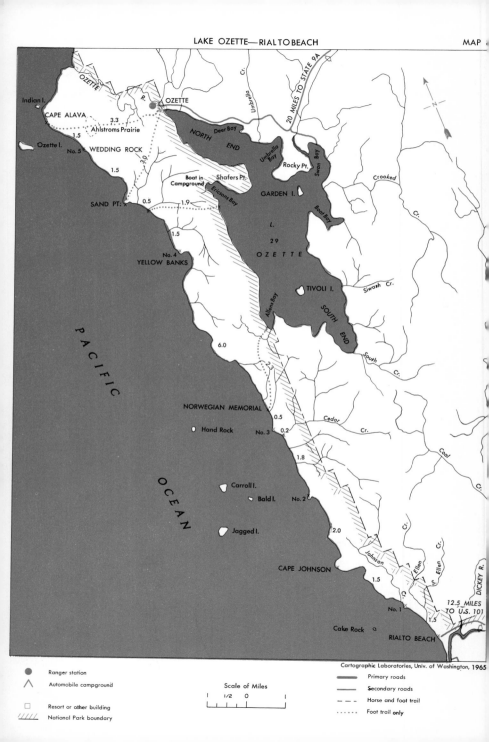

Indian I.

CAPE ALAVA

3.3

Ahlstroms Prairie

1.5

Ozette I.

No. 5   WEDDING ROCK

1.5

OZETTE

OZETTE R.

NORTH END

Deer Bay

Umbrella Cr.

20 MILES TO STATE 9A

Umbrella Bay

Rocky Pt.

Swan Bay

Crooked

Cr.

3.0

Boat in Campground

Shafers Pt.

Ericsons Bay

GARDEN I.

Boot Bay

SAND PT.

0.5

1.9

1.5

No. 4
YELLOW BANKS

L.
29

OZETTE

TIVOLI I.

Siwash Cr.

Allens Bay

SOUTH END

South

Cr.

6.0

2.3

PACIFIC

NORWEGIAN MEMORIAL

0.5

Cedar

Cr.

Hand Rock

No. 3   0.2

Coal

Cr.

1.8

OCEAN

Carroll I.

Bald I.   No. 2

Jagged I.

2.0

Johnson

Cr.

Ellen

Cr.

S. Ellen

Cr.

DICKEY R.

CAPE JOHNSON

1.5

No. 1

1.5

12.5 MILES
TO U.S. 101

Cake Rock

RIALTO BEACH

Cartographic Laboratories, Univ. of Washington, 1965

Ranger station

Automobile campground

Resort or other building

National Park boundary

Scale of Miles

1   1/2   0   1

Primary roads

Secondary roads

Horse and foot trail

Foot trail only

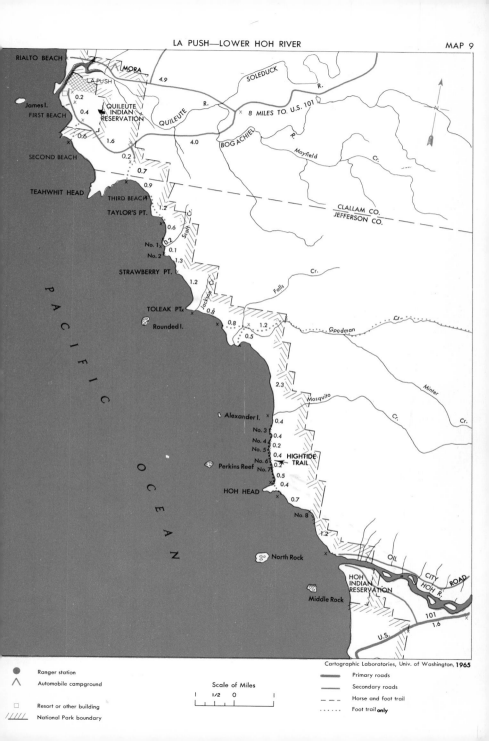

RIALTO BEACH

MORA

LA PUSH

4.9

SOLEDUCK

R.

James I.
FIRST BEACH

0.2

0.4

QUILEUTE INDIAN
RESERVATION

QUILEUTE

R.

8 MILES TO U.S. 101

0.6

1.6

4.0

BOGACHIEL

R.

Mayfield

Cr.

SECOND BEACH

0.2

0.7

0.9

TEAHWHIT HEAD

THIRD BEACH

CLALLAM CO.
JEFFERSON CO.

0.9

1.2

TAYLOR'S PT.

0.6

Scott Cr.

No. 1   0.2

No. 2   0.1
        1.3

Cr.

STRAWBERRY PT.

1.2

Jackson Cr.

Falls

TOLEAK PT.

0.8

Rounded I.

0.8

0.5

1.2

Goodman

Cr.

2.3

Minter

Mosquito

P A C I F I C

Alexander I.   0.4

No. 3   0.4

No. 4   0.2

No. 5   0.4

HIGHTIDE
TRAIL

Cr.

Cr.

No. 6   0.2

Perkins Reef   No. 7

0.5

0.4

HOH HEAD

0.7

No. 8

1.2

O C E A N

North Rock

OIL

CITY

HOH INDIAN
RESERVATION

HOH R.

ROAD

Middle Rock

101

U.S.

1.6

Cartographic Laboratories, Univ. of Washington, 1965

●   Ranger station

∧   Automobile campground

□   Resort or other building

/////   National Park boundary

Scale of Miles

1   1/2   0

Primary roads

Secondary roads

Horse and foot trail

Foot trail only

OIL CITY RD.
3.8
HOH
HOH. INDIAN RESERVATION
Braden Cr.
101
0.8
North Rock
Middle Rock
U.S. 0.8
2.1
Cedar Cr.

Abbey I.
RUBY BEACH
1.7
Sand Cr.
South Rock
Steamboat Cr.
BEACH NO. 7
0.5
BEACH NO. 6
0.6
DESTRUCTION I.
BIG CEDAR
0.3
0.6
1.1
BEACH NO. 4
0.7
BEACH NO. 3
1.6
HIGHWAY VIEWPOINT
Kalaloch Cr.
1.8
CLEARWATER R.
0.9
KALALOCH
1.0
BEACH NO. 2
0.9
CLEARWATER
BEACH NO. 1
1.2
Hurst Cr.
QUINAULT
2.0
QUEETS
INDIAN
QUEETS R.
RESERVATION
Harlow Cr.
QUEETS
7.0
Fisher Cr.
Miller Cr.

Cartographic Laboratories, Univ. of Washington, 196_

Ranger station
Automobile campground
Resort or other building
National Park boundary

Scale of Miles
1   1/2   0   1

Primary roads
Secondary roads
Horse and foot trail
Foot trail

N

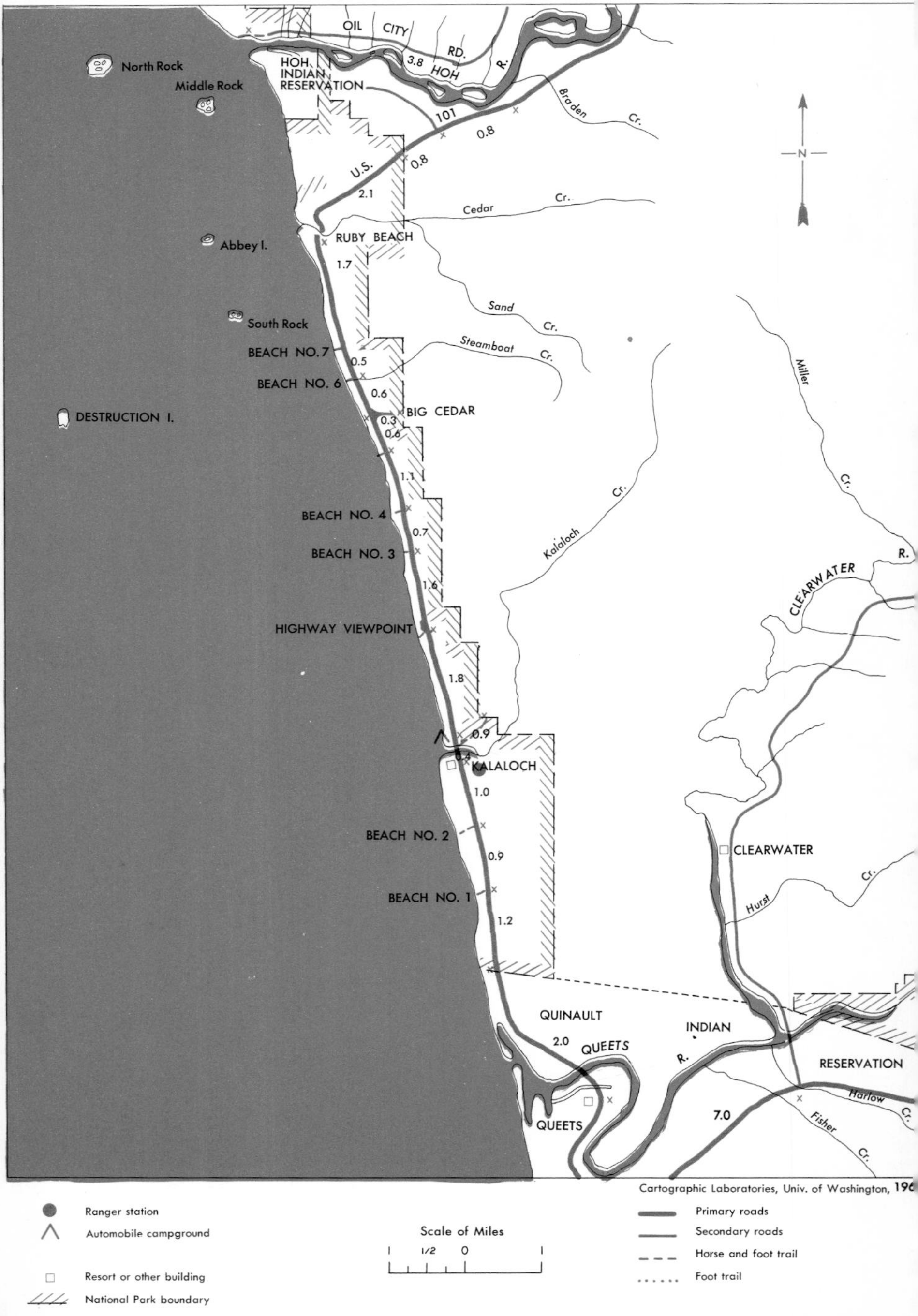

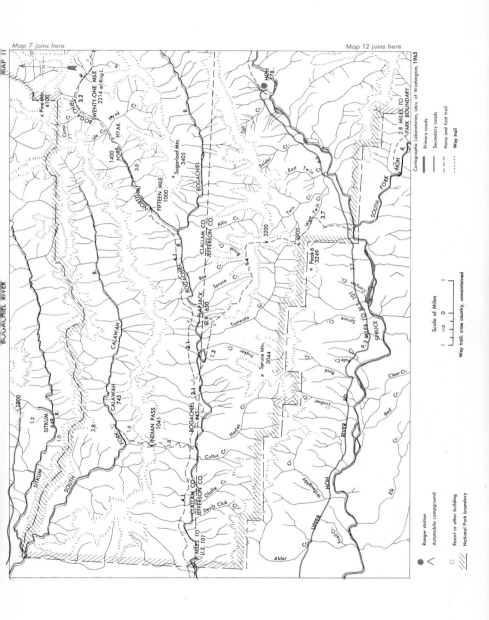

Map 7 joins here

Map 12 joins here

MAP 11

BOGACHIEL RIVER

Cartographic Laboratories, Univ. of Washington, 1965

Primary roads
Secondary roads
Horse and foot trail
Way trail

2.8 MILES TO
PARK BOUNDARY

HOH
578

SOUTH FORK

HOH R.

Scale of Miles

1/2   0   1

Way trail, cross country, unmaintained

● Ranger station
< Automobile campground
□ Resort or other building
▨ National Park boundary

x Pine Mtn.
4100

Camp Cr.

BOGACHIEL

TWENTY-ONE MILE
2214

Ring L.

Hyak Cr.

HYAK

NORTH FORK

1400

3.0

Sugarloaf Mtn.
3405

FIFTEEN MILE
1000

BOGACHIEL R.

Taft Cr.

Snider Cr.

East Twin Cr.

Twin Cr.

West Twin Cr.

3.7

Allin Cr.

x 3200

k 2000

BOGACHIEL R.

4.1

CLALLAM CO.
JEFFERSON CO.

Bee Cr.

Brush Cr.

6.4

Spruce Cr.

FLAPJACK
650

10.9

Tumwata Cr.

x Peak 6
3249

101

SPRUCE

9.3 MILES TO
U.S. 101

SITKUM

1000

1.2

SITKUM R.
648

1.0

CALAWAH

CALAWAH R.
745

2.8

SOUTH FORK

2.1

Froker Cr.

1.5

Spruce Mtn.
3044

Cole Cr.

Clear Cr.

1.6

INDIAN PASS
1041

1.8

BOGACHIEL R.
445

2.1

Hada Cr.

Cultus Cr.

Lindner Cr.

HOH

RIVER RD.

Rock Cr.

Red Cr.

CLALLAM CO.
JEFFERSON CO.

4.1

Ollalie Cr.

Devils Club Cr.

Willoughby Cr.

Elk Cr.

5.3 MILES TO
U.S. 101

LIBBER

Smith Cr.

Alder Cr.

MAP 12

HOH RIVER AND SOUTH FORK HOH RIVER

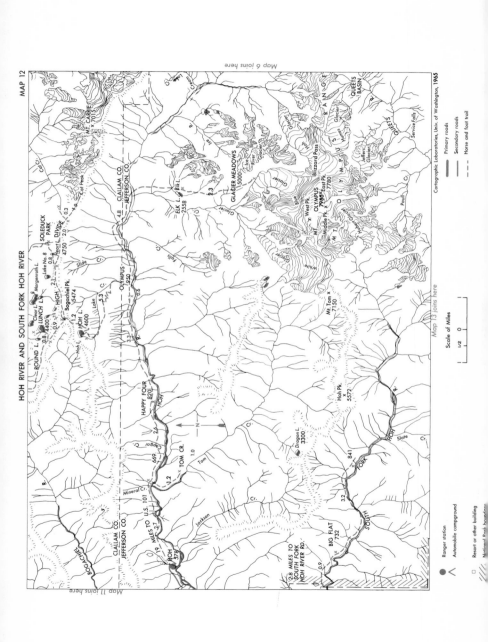

Cartographic Laboratories, Univ. of Washington, 1965

Map 6 joins here

Map 13 joins here

Map 11 joins here

Scale of Miles

1/2   0   1

Primary roads

Secondary roads

Horse and foot trail

● Ranger station

∧ Automobile campground

□ Resort or other building

National Park boundary

MT. CARRIE
x 7015

SOLEDUCK PARK

CLALLAM CO.
JEFFERSON CO.

Heart L. DIVIDE

HIGH DIVIDE

Lake No. 8

Morgenroth L.

Clear L.

ROUND L.

LUNCH L.

HIGH 4600

Bogachiel Pk.
x 5474

Earl Peak

GLACIER MEADOWS
5000

ELK L.
Elk L. 2558

OLYMPUS 950

HAPPY FOUR
820

Hoh L.

QUEETS BASIN

Service Falls

MT. OLYMPUS
7965
West Pk.
Middle Pk. x 7780
East Pk.

Blizzard Pass

Mt. Tom x
7150

Hoh Pk.
x 5572

Dragon L.
3300

Mt. Tom x

BIG FLAT
732

MILES TO
SOUTH FORK
HOH RIVER RD.

HOH 378

MILES TO U.S. 101

CLALLAM CO.
JEFFERSON CO.

Mineral Cr.

SOUTH FORK

Slate Cr.

MAP 13

QUEETS RIVER

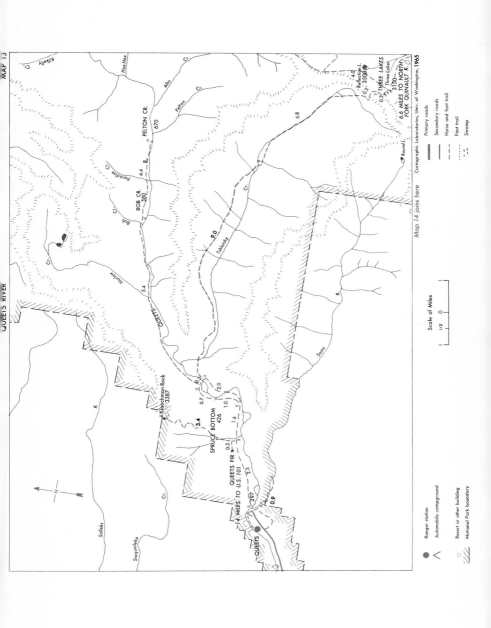

KiKelly Cr.

Hee Hee Cr.

PELTON CR.
670

Alta Cr.

Pelton Cr.

Paradise Cr.
4.4

BOB CR.
580

Bob Cr.

Horton Cr.

QUEETS R.
5.4

9.0
Tshletshy Cr.

Cr.

6.8

Round L.

4.0
Reflection L.
0.2 3500 THREE LAKES
0.3 Three Lakes
3130
6.6 MILES TO NORTH
FORK QUINAULT R.

Map 14 joins here

Sams R.

Kloochman Rock
3387

0.2
0.7 2.0
1.0
SPRUCE BOTTOM
426 1.6
3.4

QUEETS FIR
0.2
2.3

MILES TO U.S. 101

.9?
.29?
0.9

QUEETS

Sol1eks R.

Clr.

Steequaleho Cr.

N

Cartographic Laboratories, Univ. of Washington, 1965

Scale of Miles
1   1/2   0   1

Primary roads
Secondary roads
Horse and foot trail
Foot trail
Swamp

● Ranger station
∧ Automobile campground
□ Resort or other building
National Park boundary

Map 13 joins here   LAKE QUINAULT   Map 15 joins here   MAP 14

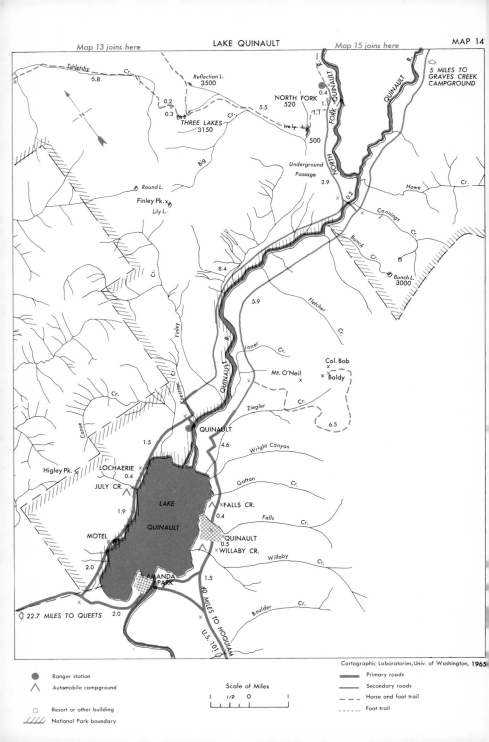

Tshletshy   Cr.
6.8

Reflection L.
3500

0.2
0.3

THREE LAKES
3150

5.5

Cr.

Irely L.

NORTH FORK
520

0.4
1.1
1.1

500

5 MILES TO
GRAVES CREEK
CAMPGROUND

NORTH FORK QUINAULT R.

QUINAULT R.

Underground
Passage
2.9

0.2

Howe   Cr.

Cannings   Cr.

Round L.

Finley Pk. x

Lily L.

Bunch   Cr.

Bunch L.
3000

8.4

Finley   Cr.

5.9

Fletcher   Cr.

QUINAULT R.

Inner   Cr.

Mt. O'Neil   x

Col. Bob
x

x Baldy

Koostner   Cr.

Ziegler

Cr.

6.5

QUINAULT

1.5

4.6

Wright Canyon

Canoe   Cr.

Higley Pk.

LOCHAERIE
0.4

JULY CR.

1.9

MOTEL

2.0

LAKE
QUINAULT

Gatton   Cr.

x FALLS CR.

0.4   Falls   Cr.

QUINAULT
0.5
x WILLABY CR.

Willaby   Cr.

AMANDA
PARK

1.5

22.7 MILES TO QUEETS   2.0

40 MILES TO HOQUIAM

U.S. 101

Boulder   Cr.

Cartographic Laboratories, Univ. of Washington, 1965

● Ranger station

∧ Automobile campground

□ Resort or other building

///// National Park boundary

Scale of Miles
1   1/2   0   1

Primary roads

Secondary roads

Horse and foot trail

.... Foot trail

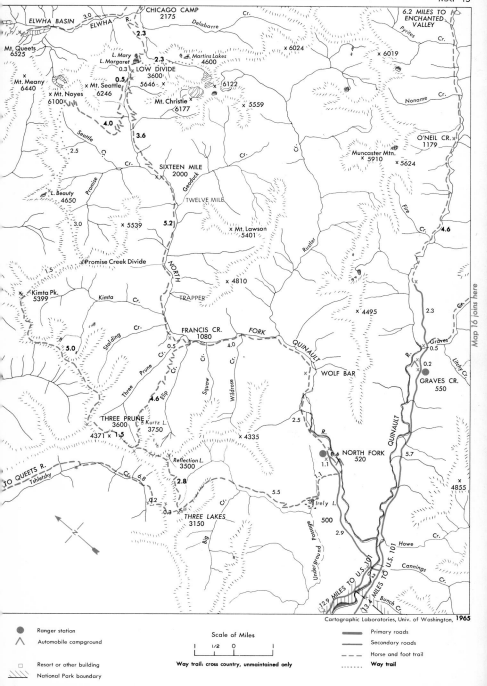

Cartographic Laboratories, Univ. of Washington, **1965**

● Ranger station	
⋀ Automobile campground	
☐ Resort or other building	
⧄ National Park boundary	

Scale of Miles

1   1/2   0   1

Way trail: cross country, unmaintained only

▬▬▬ Primary roads	
───── Secondary roads	
‒ ‒ ‒ Horse and foot trail	
······ **Way trail**	

QUINAULT RIVER—ENCHANTED VALLEY
MAP 1
Map 6 joins here
Map 2 joins here

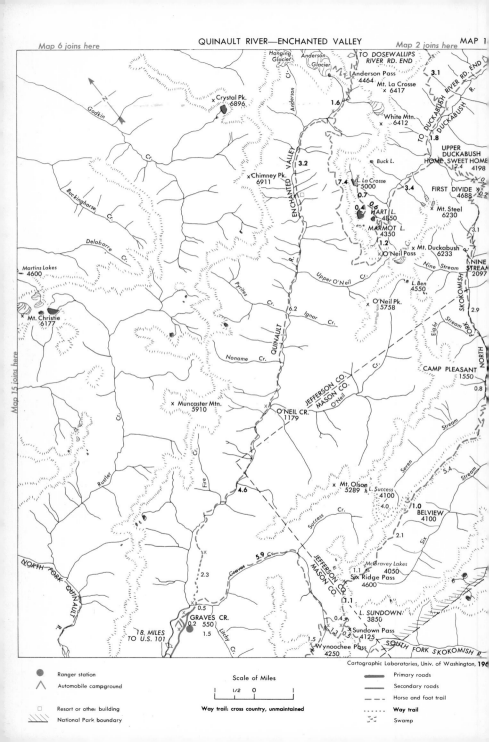

Hanging Glacier
Anderson Glacier
Anderson Cr.

TO DOSEWALLIPS RIVER RD. END

TO DUCKABUSH RIVER RD. END

3.1

Anderson Pass 4464
Mt. La Crosse x 6417

x Crystal Pk. 6896

White Mtn. 6412

1.6

1.8

UPPER DUCKABUSH HOME SWEET HOME 4198
2.4

ENCHANTED VALLEY

3.2

Buck L.

x Chimney Pk. 6911

7.4

L. La Crosse 5000

3.4

FIRST DIVIDE 4688
0.2

0.7

x Mt. Steel 6230

0.6

0.4

HART L. 4850

MARMOT L. 4350

3.1

Godkin Cr.

Buckinghorse Cr.

Delabarre Cr.

1.2

O'Neil Pass

x Mt. Duckabush 6233

NINE STREAM 2097

Upper O'Neil Cr.

Nine Stream

NORTH FORK SKOKOMISH

Martins Lakes 4600

Pyrites Cr.

L. Ben 4550

2.9

x Mt. Christie 6177

6.2

Ignar Cr.

x O'Neil Pk. 5758

QUINAULT R.

Eight Stream

Noname Cr.

Cr.

CAMP PLEASANT 1550

0.8

x Muncaster Mtn. 5910

JEFFERSON CO. MASON CO.

O'Neil Cr.

O'NEIL CR. 1179

Rustler Cr.

Fire Cr.

Seven Stream

5.4

4.6

x Mt. Olson 5289

L. Success 4100

1.0

BELVIEW 4100

4.0

2.1

Success Cr.

Six

Stream

NORTH FORK QUINAULT R.

Graves Cr.

5.9

JEFFERSON CO. MASON CO.

McGravey Lakes 4050

1.1

Six Ridge Pass 4600

2.3

18 MILES TO U.S. 101

0.5

GRAVES CR. 550
0.2

1.5

Lichy Cr.

1.1

0.4

L. SUNDOWN 3850

x Sundown Pass 4125

1.5

Wynoochee Pass 4250

SOUTH FORK SKOKOMISH R.

Cartographic Laboratories, Univ. of Washington, 196

Legend

● Ranger station

∧ Automobile campground

□ Resort or other building

National Park boundary

Scale of Miles
1/2   0

Way trail: cross country, unmaintained

Primary roads

Secondary roads

Horse and foot trail

Way trail

Swamp